Acclaimed

2011 Poetry Collection

Published by
The America Library of Poetry
P.O. Box 978
Houlton, ME 04730
Website: www.libraryofpoetry.com
Email: generalinquiries@libraryofpoetry.com

Printed in the United States of America.

THE AMERICA
LIBRARY OF POETRY

ISBN: 978-0-9773662-6-2

Contents

Poetry by Division

Acclaimed

... In memory of
Marvin Terrance Bagby and Johnathon Charles Leopold

Who Wishes To Be a Part of Violence?
by Marvin Terrance Bagby
July 9, 1996 – March 31, 2010

Who wishes to be a part of violence?
Violence is all I see
Violence is nothing but hate built up
Violence kills people
Just thinking about it could mean I am next in line
Violence is everywhere in the world
Just hearing about violence kills me inside
Violence is a big hole of darkness
Violence can make anyone do anything
Violence has people in his hand
Let's help end violence
Let us say 'no' to violence

I See a Boy
by Johnathon Charles Leopold
March 26, 1994 – May 07, 2011

I see a boy, a boy with a dream,
he dreams of becoming a hero, by joining the Marines,
he would protect our country, answer the call,
he could be a hero, by saving us all,
this calls for respect, a price he would pay,
to join the Marines, and save the day,
there would be pain, and there would be glory,
so he grabbed the horse by the mane, and started his story,
now his dream has come true, to fight for red, white, and blue,
he fights to his death, savoring every last breath,
and when his time comes, he'll get his reward,
a family that loves him, and a country that adores him,
the feeling of joy, inside that boy,
and the feeling of pride, right by his side,
kept him going until he died,
but that boy will always be remembered,
as the one who answered the call,
to join the Marines,
and save us all.

Foreword

There are two kinds of writers in the world.
There are those who write from experience,
and those who write from imagination.
The experienced, offer words that are a reflection of their lives.
The triumphs they have enjoyed, the heartaches they have endured;
all the things that have made them who they are,
they graciously share with us, as a way of sharing themselves,
and in doing so, give us, as readers, someone to whom we may relate,
as well as fresh new perspectives
on what may be our common circumstances in life.
From the imaginative,
come all the wonderful things we have yet to experience;
from sights unseen, to sounds unheard.
They encourage us to explore the limitless possibilities
of our dreams and fantasies,
and aid us in escaping, if only temporarily,
the confines of reality and the rules of society.
To each, we owe a debt of gratitude;
and rightfully so, as each provides a service of equal importance.
Yet, without the other, neither can be truly beneficial.
For instance, one may succeed in accumulating a lifetime of experience,
only to consider it all to have been predictable and unfulfilling,
if denied the chance to chase a dream or two along the way.
Just as those whose imaginations run away with them never to return,
may find that without solid footing in the real world,
life in fantasyland is empty.
As you now embark, dear reader,
upon your journey through these words to remember,
you are about to be treated to both heartfelt tales of experience,
and captivating adventures of imagination.
It is our pleasure to present them for your enjoyment.
To our many authors,
who so proudly represent the two kinds of writers in the world,
we dedicate this book, and offer our sincere thanks;
for now, possibly more than ever,
the world needs you both.

Paul Wilson Charles
Editor

Editor's Choice Award

The Editor's Choice Award is presented
to an author who demonstrates not only
the solid fundamentals of creative writing,
but also the ability to illicit an emotional response
or provide a thought provoking body of work
in a manner which is both clear and concise.

You will find "Motherhood"
by Sinnea Douglas
on page 217 of *Acclaimed*

2011
Spirit of Education

For Outstanding Participation

Garfield
Middle School

Hamilton, Ohio

Presented to participating students and faculty
in recognition of your commitment
to literary excellence.

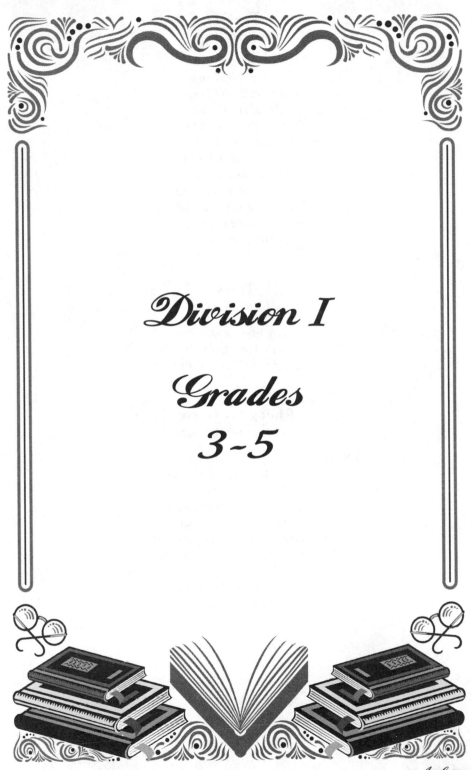

Division I

Grades
3-5

The Sun
by Grace Boyd

As the sun shines down
like a spotlight on me,
The sun is all I see.
The sun is like a ray
That brings the world light,
The sun leaves during the night.
The sun is the path
that leads me to all,
The sun is round and tall.
The special sun has a name
His name is Fun,
This is my Sun.

Trees
by Jordyn Schenck

trees, trees come alive
reach your branches to the sky
stretch out don't be shy.

Riding My Horse
by Nicole Scarbrough

When I am on my horse I feel like I am free.
The wind whipping my hair around
When galloping through the woods.
The heat beating toward me.
Sweat on my forehead.
The horse is ready for any obstacles.
We stop at the horse's favorite place.
It's a large, hidden apple tree in the woods.
I pick the ripest apples on the tree.
We eat as a snack.

Feelings
by Shelby Antonic

Roses are red,
Violets are blue.
When I see butterflies I think of you,
I think of you every day and night.
When I go to bed I have scary frights,
So I wake up and turn on the light.
In the morning I seem tired,
And if I get to work late I might get fired.
When I go walking in the park,
I hear the dogs bark.
Then I saw a girl,
She lit up my world.
I started blushing,
When I went over there I was rushing.
My heart was beating fast,
I think I might blast.

Waves
by Alexander Bradin

Big crashing waves calm
Relaxing sleepy noises
Love love ocean love

Look Towards Japan
by Madelyn Domagala

The spring breeze made the cherry trees sway,
For that was the only sound that day,
The earthquake shook the ground too much,
Leaving Japan with crumbled buildings and such,
Though crumbled houses did remain,
But then they all got swept away,
A tsunami came and it was painful to see,
Even for children like you and me,
Let's keep the Japanese in our prayers,
And give them each all of our care,
No matter how small or big or strong or fast,
In a few years Japan will all be rebuilt at last.

My Little Sister
by Devin Wierima

I have a little sister
Whose name is Sophia
She is two years old

Wal-Mart
by Ronal Gomez

I buy all my clothes at Wal-Mart
I don't buy dumb I buy smart
walking down the aisle with my shopping cart eating my smore-flavored Pop-Tart
the candy aisle with kids asking why
come on mom it's just a dollar ninety nine
I want candy I want candy
don't buy it for sista Mandy
cause I just want the candy
just put it in my handy

Burt
by Nathan Omodt

I know a shark named Burt,
When he bites you it really hurts,
He likes to stab things with a stick,
He does it with his best friend Moby Dick,
Once they bit off a lion's mane,
They always stop biting when it starts to rain,
When you go swimming watch your feet,
These are two animals you don't want to meet!

Like Glass
by Madison Glenn

Friendship is like glass.
Strong and yet it will break on impact.
You can do your best to put it back together.
You will still see all the cracks and flaws things that can never be repaired.
You will be forced to watch the pieces fall to the ground
as you grow further and further apart.
Until one day you see them
all scattered on the ground ... forgotten

Roses
by Artina Li

In my sight there's a field of flowers,
I loved them because of their special colors.
Dancing in the sunlight as the wind blew,
Bowed when hit by the wind and let it flow.
Enduring smell, perfume in a lady's hair,
grandeur but fragile in need of dainty care.
When it's time, you know why,
Time to plant more when they say goodbye!

Hibiscus
by Sydney Antczak

Hibiscus
Orange and yellow
Dewdrops falling slowly
Beautiful tropical plant
Flower

With a Road Right Beside Me
by Katelynn Boyd

With a road right beside me
and the cars passing by,
The birds fly over
There is not even a sigh.
As the wind picks up
and the trees start to sway,
The flowers begin to bloom
and my dog comes this way.
As I sit on this fence post
looking up at the sky,
I look at the shapes of the clouds
Up so very high.
The bikers biking by
with a squirrel following behind,
Wish I had that courage
Still need to find.
With a road right beside me
and the cars passing by,
The birds fly over
There is not even a sigh.

4, 3, 2, 1
by Bryan Lovell

4, 3, 2, 1 look at me I am on the sun.
5, 4, 3, 2 look at me I am in a shoe.
6, 5, 4, 3 look at me I am in a tree.
7, 6, 5, 4 look at me I am on the floor.
8, 7, 6, 5 look at me I am in a beehive.

Football
by Noah Paulseth

Football
Quarterback, receiver
It is fun
Fun for quarterbacks
Watch

Dolphins
by Madisen Paulseth

Sitting along the shore watching dolphins splish and splash.
Watching the beautiful sea flowing in the breeze.
My laughter sparkles like a splash of water in sunlight as I watch the dolphins play.
For I love how graceful the dolphins are.
I love the sea so much.
I never want to leave!

My School
by Matty Robson

I like my school,
it really rules.
All my friends here,
are all cool!
Our school is closing,
we all are sad.
But we are friends,
and that's really rad!!!

Pride
by Paolo Orosa

If pride were a color, it would be purple.
Pride tastes like bitter beer.
Pride sounds like Kanye West bragging.
Pride smells like a wet dog.
Pride looks like a peacock strutting.
Pride makes me feel selfish and arrogant.

The Fair
by Isabella Anger

There once was a girl who had a teddy bear
She said to her father can we please go to the fair
It costs no money
No, not now, honey
But I absolutely have to go there!

Fly
by Sarabeth Walker

There was a fly,
He landed on my thigh,
I screamed and I ran to my mom,
Then I ran to my brother, Tom.
The fly followed me there,
So I threw underwear.
The fly stayed right there with a sigh,
With his wicked little eye, one cry,
He told me he didn't have fear.
I didn't believe him so I looked at his rear,
His rear has a tattoo of a fear.
I gasped and I said, "My dear, you do have a fear it's a puppeteer."
"Yes," said the fly, "It's really the puppets that scare me,
They have big ears, big eyes, and tiny mouths like a hole,
And their nose is just 'Ih'."
Then I felt like doing something, something that not everybody does,
I felt like chasing the fly.
A grin appeared, he looked at me weird,
for smiling in an odd sort of way.
I jumped up and started to run,
He flew as fast as he could,
Then he said, "I take it back, I have two fears. YOU!" he shouted.

Nature Around Us
by Maryam Alwan

Nature controls everything in its path, how ominous
To us, many of its creatures are anonymous
From the birds to the trees, and the ants to the bees
The world is full of surprises
Storms too, like tsunamis, how ferocious
The only ones who survive are courageous
Many happen on the Pacific
It's scary, it's horrific
But that's how the world goes 'round
From Haiti to Japan
And the flooding Nile in Sudan
Nature affects us all
There are also Hurricanes
They happen along the Texas plains
Wind is creepy after all
Very similar, there are tornadoes
These might happen in Idaho, the land of potatoes
Soaring high, in the sky
Or close to the ground below
Nature leaves you in awe.

Tornado
by Jett Alexander Shue

Whipping up a twirling path;
showing off its windy wrath.
Ever twirling round and round;
tearing up the grassy ground.
Up I go, through the funnel;
Pulls me, devours me, in the tunnel.
Its eye is blind, but the beast will hurt
as it combines my skin with grass and dirt.
White hot needles pierce my skin;
In this battle I cannot win.
Finally, when it is done,
We clean, rebuild, and have some fun!

Every Day
by Alexa Pongratz

Every day I wake up it's the same routine!
Brush my teeth real good,
brush my hair to look like a fashion model!
Put on some good clothes,
grab my backpack and I'm ready to go!
Ooooo!
I leave school feelin' confident that today's gonna be the day
that I'll finally say hello to you without my face turnin' red!
Yeah, yeah, yeah!
I'm feelin' pretty confident!
When I walk into the classroom, I get so nervous
that I can't hear myself think over the noise of my heart beatin'!
People start starin' at me like I'm some kind of nasty old animal species!
They don't like my clothes they don't get my hair.
No, no, no! I can't do this!

Mother
by Jayda Smith-Redding

You are my
mother
also my friend
you
bring me joy
until
the end. I
know
I bring you
joy
too. Remember
this
your whole life
through.
I love you.

The Cave of a Wave
by Ryleigh Katstra

Never mind the trees swaying.
Never mind the sand blowing.
But when a wave comes crashing down,
When I have my back turned,
It opens up like a cave,
like a cave.

Life Is a Maze
by Keeli Bowles

Life. Life is a maze.
Life is a maze filled with twists
and turns and dead ends.
But eventually we all
will finish the maze.

Stalking Tiger
by Alex Knodel

I crept forward, blood tingling, claws extended,
Stomach growling softly, ready to pounce.
A full-grown gazelle close to me, walking with a limp.
The gazelle could not see me in the tall, hazy, brown grass.
I prepared myself, ready to strike at any moment.
I leaped forward, aimed at the gazelle, flying through the air.
Thud!!!
I hit the gazelle and it dropped.
It was all over so quickly.
Now it is time to eat the warm, fresh meat.
My job is done.
I am satisfied.

The Book We All Read
by Maddy Settel

Let the pages be worn,
Let the pages be tattered,
Devour the pages and know the knowledge,
Keep it by your heart.
You shall read the book over and then again.
Shall the words be spoke out?
Not to a soul, not one.
Keep reading, you shall see the end.
Soon.

Waves
by Devin Granata

The waves crashing down
It feels like a paradise
A life with great fun.

Spring Nature
by Alyssa Asbury

Watch as the birds fly branch to branch.
Watch as mother duck swims happily with her young following.
Watch the butterflies and their beautiful wings.
Just sit and watch in this beautiful peace.
Watch as the horses run in the sunset.
Watch all the fire flies in the night sky.
Watch a spring day begin
and say goodbye.

Dr. Seuss Rhyme
by Roger Harris III

Dr. Seuss is the best author,
He made the Cat in the Hat,
You know you can't dis that.
He rhymes so good that he can't waste your time,
Thing 1, Thing 2, you can't miss that rhyme.
If we ran the cicus we will read all day,
Dr. Seuss books will never go away.
I had trouble running the circus,
But Mulberry Street gave me the purpose.
Dr. Seuss, you the man,
We are your number one fans!!!!!

The Cold Weather
by Bailey Ranstrom

It is frosty outside
It is cold outside with frost
No one likes to go outside

Blue
by Kate Wagner

Blue is the color of water sloshing over your feet on the beach.
It is the dolphins jumping out of the water on a clear spring day.
Blue is the color of a robin's eggs.
It is the blue birds singing their beautiful song in the early spring.
Blue is the color of the clear sky on a warm summer's day.

Moon
by Andrea Garcia-Gamez

Lovely and shining
Rising after the sun set
Lovely shining moon

Baby
by Grant Leshovsky

Baby
Brown hair, Blue eyes
Smiles and talks
Hold, change diapers
Holden

A Guy Once Said, "Hi"
by Devin Dukes

A guy once said, "Hi"
He liked to eat pie
He liked it a lot
He never let it rot
And he never tells a lie

Friendship
by Kayla Mercer

A friend is like the sun
They shine on you
A friend is like a new toy
You hold it close
A friend is like candy
Sweet and lasting
A friend is like glasses
They help you see clear
A friend is like the earth
They surround you
Where would we be if there wasn't a friend?

Fun, Fun, Fun
by William Simms III

Fun, Fun, Fun,
Spring and playing in the sun.
Fun, Fun, Fun,
Winter is done.
Fun, Fun, Fun,
Come play everyone.

Peter McChuck
by Logan Gunther

There once was a duck
His name was Peter McChuck
He got distracted by a plane
And his life was never the same
Because he landed in a pile of muck.

Kirby
by Alex Walker

Kirby
My dog
A vacuum cleaner
Loves to take walks
Barks

Life
by David Lyon

Beauty is seen in the greenhouse.
Lady slippers swaying in a gust of wind.
Vines standing erectly over the wall.
Roses poking each other and hindering their growing pace.
Tulips blooming into their beautiful brethren.
Dragonflies showing their beauty to the world.
Bees sucking the nectar out of their helpless victims.
Morning glories and their unbearable beauty.
Beauty is heard at the greenhouse.
Rain tapping on the window.
The gentle wailing of wind.
Water being expelled from the rest.
Laughter from kids on a field trip.
Wailing of the kids when they touch the prickly stems of the beautiful roses.
The"caching"of the register when mothers check out their items.
Beauty is in yourself.
A great personality.
Making people laugh.
Showing charity for people in need.
Being a good person in the world.
Helping out your community.
And most of all,
LOVE

Chameleon
by Brandon Heikell

Chameleon, chameleon, where are you?
I looked behind the lion's cage and by the kangaroo.
Chameleon, chameleon, where are you?
Are you in the city or are you in the zoo?
Chameleon, chameleon, where are you?
Are you in Bethesda or maybe Baton Rouge?
Chameleon, chameleon, where are you?
Are you in America or possibly Peru?
Oh no! What if chameleon's dead?
What? You say he's on top of my head?
Chameleon, chameleon, I found you!

My Friend Wizzy
by Philip Hart

My friend Wizzy was feeling dizzy.
He was fast but got stuck in the past.

A Trip To the Blue Ridge Mountains
by Angie Wang

From far away these mountains are blue,
The mist wraps itself, around this beautiful view.
A sparrow chirps its welcoming call,
That travels over the clear streams, down the veil-like waterfall,
Over the golden valley,
Across the grassy meadow, and I hear the sweet melody.
I feel the gentle breeze
As it weaves through the trees.
I see the birds fly
Beneath the fluffy clouds in the sky.
I breathe in the pine-filled smell,
Now I don't want to say farewell.
Before I go,
My gaze traveled across the grassy meadow,
Over the golden valley, down the veil-like waterfall,
Over the crystal clear streams, and rested on the small sparrow that made the call.
But this time it said, "See you around!"
I smiled and left the Blue Ridge Mountains
With happiness that I just found.

Monkeys
by Shayna Syverson

Monkeys move wildly
they love to eat bananas
and jump to each branch
laughing at each other's fun
they are a very dark brown.

Inside This Chest
by Brendan Deller

Inside this chest
Is fun and happiness
And friendship for all
It says, "That Jesus will guide us."
That's what it says at the bottom of the chest
Inside this chest
Is the Holy Trinity
They will guide us through all things
When we have trouble in life
They will be with us forever
Inside this chest
Is everything good
And nothing bad
Like love and peace
Throughout the world

Outer Space Aliens
by Cora McQuaid

One day when I was in outer space
I went face to face with an alien
on its outer space base.
I told him his shoelace was undone
but he didn't believe me so when he
tried to take a step he landed face to face
on his alien base in outer space.

Peppy
by Paige Whittaker

Peppy's tail swishes and sways,
Out in the pasture, not in the stalls.
He sighs and he whinnies; his stride steady
As every hoofbeat falls.
After galloping and loping all day
The smell of sweat and hay fill the air.
A strong but gentle gelding,
Happy and confident, I haven't a care!

Wild Flowers!
by Rhaven Ransaw

On the side of the road are wild flowers.
They start to bloom after April showers.
You can pick a bunch to make a bouquet.
Then give it to someone to brighten their day.
When wild flowers bloom they make me sneeze.
Blowing left to right in the cool breeze.
Some are skinny some are small.
It does not matter because I like them all.
They are different colors yellow, white, and blue.
I think they're pretty what about you?

Lions
by Linnea Bollum

Lions they are really fierce
With their claws they can pierce
They are fast and jumpy
They are always grumpy
I like that lions are fierce

The Cat
by Grace Joy

Inside this hat
I found a cat
It started to purr
It got ruffles on its fur
Oh I want him to go
But he can't it started to snow
I don't want him to freeze
20 below that's just the breeze
I tried to give him food
I think he's just in a bad mood
I think he misses his mother
So I do not want to be a bother
I love him so much
I will never feed him mush
I named him Tom
I will always be his mom

My Pig
by Danielle Crouch

Someday I will get a pig.
Her name will be Fig.
I hope she likes to jig,
And put on a wig.
Perhaps she'll like to dig.

Summer
by Michael Woodard

Summer
fun, hot
Candy, flame
Scaring, screaming, laughing
Crazy, cool
Halloween

Spring
by Jim Coulter

April showers
Bring May flowers
Out comes the sun
Time for fun
Spring is here
The best time of the year
The grass is green
The best thing I've seen
The bees are buzzing
And we are running
Run, run from the bees
Get away, climb up the trees
I really do not like those bees
The weather is hot
I go outside a lot
Get rid of those sweatshirts
Put on those t-shirts
It is spring
Time to sing
Spring is the best time of the year

Fall Poem
by Evan Cordrey

Fall is great
Fall is fun
I think I need a little sun
October is great
It's the best
Halloween's mate
It's a fest
The leaves fall
We have a ball
You can't get enough of fall
Rake the leaves into a pile
Jump in them and give a smile
The days get shorter
The nights get longer
It is cold
And I am getting old.

The Life of Nature
by Dale Garrett

From the soil a plant grows
Maybe in a fret
To see its bros
Don't go and make a bet
It rises higher and higher
To reach the sky
Don't set it on fire
Don't bake it into a pie
As it reaches an end
It comes to peace
It may go and mend
Let's not make it the least

Kittens
by Brian Rollison

Kittens brown and soft
They sneak past the sleeping hound
Kittens sly and smart

The Bug
by Gabrielle Vetter

There once was a bug
who was stuck to a mug
That bug sure could sting
said the owner Mr. Fling
He poured some coffee
then grabbed some toffee
Down his throat
The bug did float. Ugh!!

A New Hope
by David Newton

As I was watching the sky I saw the soaring eagle,
I saw the flesh-eating vultures and the fast falcon.
I saw a helpless blue-jay with a broken wing ... fluttering.
I saw a tangled butterfly, helplessly ... struggling to be free from the spider's web,
but did not even know he was making it worse.
Then I caught a glimpse of myself fighting for a new hope.
I then found God, and He gave me that hope.

Bad Bee
by Tomas Vivas

There once was a big bad bee,
Who lived in a big green tree.
If you break his wings,
He comes over and stings.
Then you'll get a big health insurance fee.

It's Time To Pray
by Jordan Romnes

It's the end of the day and it's time to pray for all the things that happened today.
For the flowers, to the rain, and the sunshine to the animals.
Also pray for the world at night.
Now I'm done and I am ready to say ...
Amen

Football
by Marshall Ness

Football is hard work
Passing, hiking, and running
I am a player

Webkinz
by Christiane Palmer

They are like fluffy cotton candy
They are squishy marshmallows
They keep you warm in wintertime
They are soft and cuddling animals
They keep the bad dreams away
They cost money to get them
This is a Webkinz

Strong, Weak, and Great To Eat
by Cahlin Clow

Northerns are strong, Sunnies are weak
And Walleyes are just great to eat.

Moods of All Americans
by MacKenzie Otkin

The American mind is great and full of wonder.
Moods are forever changing, mad to happy.
These are the moods of a teacher.
The adult mind is in work all day.
Stressed to calm.
Their moods change.
Some are different than others.
The one with most ever changing moods
is the president. He goes from stern to silly
yes even him.
Kids also have mood swings. That's not hard to believe.
We go from scared to brave.
Teens are even moodier.
They go from nice to mean just like that.
Today my mood is dark like a cloud over my head.
But who knows that tomorrow I could just be glad.

Vampires Rule
by Courtney Nunnelley

There was a vampire
Who ruled over an empire
He always sucked blood
From people with floods
He never dare kiss a she-vampire

Frog Food
by Trevor Brezen

I'm a bumpy clumpy old frog
I think I'm going to die I need to catch flies
I lie, lie, lie until I see a fly
I wait, wait, wait until I see my bait
I sit, sit, sit until I think I can hit
I stay, stay, stay until I see my prey
I'm still, still, still until ...
Crunch, munch, crunch, munch
mmmm ... tasty bug extract

I'm From
by Ella Busch

I'm from a family of 4, Mommy's little girl.
The harsh separation we shared for a year,
my sister too young to know, but yet I feared.
I'm from a small town with walk-to places, I always see the same faces.
A street with friends near and far.
I'm from sports everyday–basketball, soccer too much to say.
The games, swim meets, and tournaments every weekend.
I'm from relatives far away only to visit on holidays.
I do get cards and letters from them too.
I'm from pets, pets, and PETS!!!!!! Hamsters, dogs, and fish but much more in store.
I'm from a strict family but I do adore.
Also a sister who's mean and loving, sometimes.
Young to old, past to present, I will still be who I am today.

Queen
by Katie Lose

Standing out
From all the others
Perfectly shaped face
Containing the expression of a queen
I can see wisdom
In the depths
Of your emerald eyes
Feathery tail
Flowing downward
Like a river
Neat fur
White fur with large splashes
Of inky black
Joined by rings of silver
I miss your trust
You will stay with me
Like a scar etched in my palm
–For Sabrina, 2002-2010

Slow Pain
by John Graves-Marchand

In the mist below the ocean
A cry rings out
A young whale's mom is killed
Now the young one must go
To see the same fate of his mom
When the young whale comes
He feels much pain
Then his life flashes
A harpoon has lunged through him
The whale dead before the flash
He wail's one more cry
A cry of pain

Money
by Nikolaus Hochsprung

Money
Love it
Always spending it
Bills paper pennies copper
Bankrupt

Something Cute
by Emma Reed

Cute
so cuddly
very very playful
they are great pets
kittens.

It's Only a Dream
by Frank Ways

I dreamed a dream with a terrible scene; I wish I could go back and change.
With giant spiders and evil clowns and things I cannot say.
It was a game that ended with pain, and I was glad I woke up.
It happened again my terrible fate so creepy so scary I could not wake,
but I decided to go through the gate of the fearless.
So I ran from my fate and aimed toward the gate.
I ran I jumped I tripped when I ducked but somehow I managed to stay alive.
I swept through the gate away from my fate still hoping I wouldn't die.
But I wasn't prepared for what was next,
it happened so fast I couldn't revolve to see.
The dream knew I didn't conquer my fear so it sent a test, it sent the best.
A creature with six arms and legs and was surely a pest
(that the exterminators couldn't get)
I ran I jumped I hit a tree stump and flipped right over it.
I peeked from behind my protection and what I saw messed up my digestion,
my foe got a new toy a huge sword and boy was it sharp.
I screamed at it, it beamed at me, I hide behind a big oak tree,
I felt my tears dribble heavier than rocks and whisper, "it's only a dream."
I whispered what they said, "it's only a dream."

Reading
by Caitlyn Jacobson

Reading
Fun, boring
Words, chapters, crazy
Never stop going
READ

Bob
by Kelsey Lorenz

Bob
Hairy, soft
Cute and cuddly
Brown with pink ears
Bear

Surprise In the Sky
by Kenneth Spitzley IV

One night I took a pole and a hook
to go fishing in the brook.
I saw a fish swim by.
It looked like it was in the sky.
Then I looked up and saw something shine.
I took a sling shot made from a pine.
I shot it then it came tumbling down,
falling, falling to the ground.
It all happened after the crash,
when he came down in a flash.
I decided to help him fix the ship,
and he was so happy he started to skip.
When I was done he gave me a prize,
He said that I was very wise.
I told him thank you for the gift,
as the UFO began to lift.
The alien hopped in and flew really high,
higher and higher, into the sky.
I told him bye, please come again.
He said okay, with a grin.

Dreams
by Monique Kapila

I wish at night when we are asleep
Where we can find ourselves in our dreams
A time when you can feel safe to think what you want
Feel free with your own expression
Your own thoughts
Nobody can control who you want to be
But they can influence you into thinking you want to be
someone else
It's all up to you and who you choose to listen to
Your heart or your mind
But after all the commotion of life
You will always have your dreams
Whether at night or your aspirations

Christopher Columbus
by Carl WM. Del Solar Carrier

I'm Christopher Columbus,
I sail the ocean blue,
When I came back I saw a lot of glue,
So here I am on the island,
Looking for someone to sue,
And then I hired a lawyer
And sued him too!

What a Notebook Likes To Eat
by Aleeya Ghafoor

for breakfast a notebook likes to eat pencil lead with some pen ink
for a little snack a notebook would like some eraser shavings, yum!
for lunch marker ink is fine because you notebook needs some taste
for dinner letters are fine. it'll make your notebook very smart and full
that's what a notebook likes to eat.

Sam and His Friend
by Brandon Miller

There once was a lamb
He went to the shed to get the cam
He saw his friend Sam
When they got back they ate ham
Then they went to Grand Slam

A Night In My Bed
by Frey Berge

I see my bed, I see my life. It's as happy as ever, but not quite right.
I see there, I see here, my stuffed animals sleeping tight,
but my seal, my turtle, nor my shark being happy, but not quite right.
They are sleeping with sadness somehow.
I can see their tears, I can see no light, they have no love,
but then I crawled closer and gave them a big warm hug.
I feel their feelings with the big warm hug,
they are being happy and I feel a lot of love.

He Made It That Way
by Claire Rooney

How do the planets know how to orbit?
How do the stars know how to shine?
How do the clouds know how to open?
And how to let their water pour on?
How do they know when they are empty?
How do the frogs know how to croak?
How do the plants know how to grow?
How do the birds know how to fly?
And know east from west?
How do they know to sing their song?
Who knew to make them just know?
How does a rabbit know how to hop?
How does a porcupine know how to defend itself?
How does a bee know how to buzz?
And know to sting?
How do they know how to make honey?
How do our brains know how to think?
And our hearts to beat?
Who, who made them that way?
God.

Anything Can Happen Inside My Dreams
by Katey Jewett

Anything can happen inside my dreams ...
Like a cat who is surfing under the sea
Like an octopus sky diving
A squirrel who likes hang gliding
Or a dog that is riding a flea
Anything can happen inside my head ...
Like an ostrich that's sleeping under my bed
Like a monkey who's skateboarding
A dog who is snowboarding
Or a bird who is teaching Phys. Ed.

My Brother
by Taylor Gunn

My Brother is the sweetest, meanest.
But the cutest brother in the world
He can be glum, but say hi.
And he can play all day.
He can love me but he can hate me.
But we know we are always
Brother and sister.

I Wish
by Dylan Lewis

I wish I was in Afghanistan
Raising the American Flag
Peace and happiness all around
the soldiers finally come home
No more nuclear threats

Opener of Deer Hunting
by Zeth Schmidtke

It is the day of deer hunting,
My dad and I haven't seen a deer.
It's 11:50, we are going to go.
My dad whispers to me buck.
He didn't think I could get up fast enough
So he shoots first then I do.
It falls down to the ground and wiggling
My dad gets down to kill it
when he was walking I shot it in the leg
We got it after six shots.
It was only 5 points
it was good enough for my first deer.

Skiing
by Lachlan Larson

Gliding, you belong with air
Click, click shoes on skis
Ready to go again–fast

Heavenly Protectors
by Erin Boehme

Jeweled protectors of the night
Shimmering angels taking flight
Longing for the light of day
Reaching for it but kept at bay
Singing about the isles of light
But kept in the world of forever night
Keeping alive the dreams and hopes
Of condemned souls tied in devil's ropes
Waiting for the day to come
When they will be released from
Their endless toils in the night
To release the souls from their plight

Havoc
by Zachary Short

This war is bloodshed; pain in every soldier.
Men fighting for independence.
Red against blue; a milestone in history.
A milestone for all soldiers.
This war is endless; soldiers lacking sleep.
If one sleeps, one gets killed.
This war is lasting forever!
Happiness inside; hate outside.
This war has finally ended.
Many men down
Independence being declared, although we stand among the dead.
Rest in peace all those once fighting, now dead.
Our future is in question.
What will come?
We sleep with independence but also fear of the unknown.
Will we all die?
Will we remain a nation?
Independence is ours; but what about strength?
We will grow throughout the years; we will build a community.
We will live a new life, celebrate our independence, and love our new nation!

My Dog Ate Barbie!
by Emma Riedel

My Dog ate Barbie!
It all started when I saw something that looked like a peg,
It was her shoe!
Then I saw the dog picking his teeth with her leg!
Then I saw Ken shed a tear.
He said, "I'm all alone over here!"
Then my dog began to laugh,
When I said some words on her behalf.
"She was getting old anyway."
Maybe it was for the best ...
Because the dog looked at Ken,
Licked his chops,
And said, "YOU'RE NEXT!"
Ken hoped for survival,
While thinking of his arrival,
To the big toy box in the sky!

Collards
by Whitney Hopson

When I eat collards
they make me holler.
Oh yes, they are so delicious
when it's all gone I turn vicious.
Collards are so good you should try them.
They make your mouth slobber for more.

Winter
by Lydia Endalkachew

I love winter as much as I love summer.
There are kids skiing, snowboarding, sledding, ice skating, and figure skating.
Kids are also making snowmen and having snowball fights.
Us kids play in the snow for hours and hours 'till the day is done.
As we say "goodnight" or "see ya tomorrow"
we still want to have more fun in the snow, and were filled with sorrow.
When we all get home, we could see through our windows,
that the air is getting colder ... and colder.
We can also see the wind blowing harder ... and harder.
After we wash up, play some games, and snuggle by the fire,
drinking hot chocolate, waiting for dinner
we all talk or do something as a family together.
Dinner is ready!
We all talk about our day, what we did, and having a great time together.
We're all done, and it's family game and movie night!
We all play board games, and watch a couple movies.
We all had a great time together as a family and it's time for bed.
After a long day in the cold snow, and having a lot of fun,
we're all finally tucked in warm and cozy beds.
With a candle flickering by my bedside table, I look at the night sky,
wondering if the aunt I never met is looking at me with welcoming eyes
saying, "Good night and go to sleep sweetheart."
I look at the stars trying to hide my sadness.
Then I see the stars forming into something at first I didn't understand.
Then I finally saw what she was trying to tell me for the past few days.
The stars formed two words, and it said, "Merry Christmas!"
At what I saw I finally closed my eyes and I fell asleep,
dreaming about what Christmas would be like with her in person.

Fall
by Jason Tischler

Fall wakes
Trees darken
Fall runs, harvesting the plants
Withering leaves
Lighting the trees with red,
green,
orange,
yellow,
and brown.
Getting prepared for hibernation
stocking up on food
Cheeks filled with nuts
Jackets on kids as they are raking leaves.

Our Little Barn
by Grace Lech

Our little barn,
Sitting on a flat land.
All white metal sides,
Like a little house by our house.
A home to eleven pets.

Friends For Life
by Taylor Hampton

Friends are people you can't live without.
When you need an ear or a shoulder to cry a friend is near.
Friends are there ... on the tough days, on the good days, and all the days in between.
They will laugh, they will play, they will sing, and dance all with just you.
Young or old friends make life easier and give it meaning.

The Muddy Boots
by Mikayla Norton

As my muddy boots stomp on the ground
I hear the sounds of gun shots.
Pow! Pow! Pow!
And the bloody murder screams of soldiers
Help! Help! Help!

Day and Night
by Efrata Tecle

Day is the time to laugh and play!
Kids shout and scream hurray!
The sun is so bright you don't need another light!
But sooner or later it turns into night!
During the night it may give you a fright.
But the stars and the moon are shining so bright!
Telling you to stay you start to dream of the bay
You feel hazy and lazy.
Then you start to take flight.
Into the beautiful dreams of day and night!

God
by Jordan Gray

God is great he loves us all
He loves the short he loves the tall
He loves the young he loves the old
He loves us like we love gold
He loves all his creations all the animals and all the trees
he loves all the insects even the bees.

Victory
by Trinity Jelinek

Pow, Pow, Pow, shots being fired for victory
Everyone wants liberty
I am in much agony
My hope is low
but I am fearless
As bombs burst in the air
Our future is dependent on this war
Lights, flash before my eyes
Compassion fills the air
Independence!

Day and Night
by Wyneth Thompson

As daylight crumbles,
the moonlight forms
and the clouds go away.
And then, before you know it,
the stars come out to play.

Seasons
by Rachel Lowery

Every year four seasons go by
You can sometimes see them in the sky
Winters are so cold
But spring is always so bold
Summer is so hot
Fall is really not
So every year four seasons go by
You can see them if you try

Silver Twilight
by Chamber Lucas

Her soft glow,
it whispers slowly to me,
she rises up at the darkest hour,
only showing her partial beauty,
every now and then,
she'll reveal herself,
her full truancy,
now, at silver twilight,
she disappears,
from the eye for now,
but never from my soul.

In the Field of Wheat
by Jacob Deuell

In a field of wheat
Antelope play with the cows
Eating very good treats.

Football
by Harrison Nord

Football is a sport
You can throw or kick the ball
In a stadium.

Wild Pansies
by Sadie Van Wie

Wild pansies dancing
The sun making its way through the trees
Wild pansies prancing
Meadows are greener that ever before
Dandelions turn white
Then start the cycle over once more
Creating fields of yellow sunlight
The rain won't hurt you
It just makes everything look more beautiful
The bees won't cause death
They just make sure the flowers keep blooming
There may be storms
There may be droughts
But those aren't forever
Pretty soon it will all clear up
And you'll be back to the beginning
With no worries and no fears
With no stress and a free mind
Outside in the sun or rain
It's still spring and you know it
Because the wild pansies are in bloom.

The Monarch's Flight
by Greta Linder

A butterfly soars,
A cardinal flaps her wings,
The wind takes me by the hand and says come with me,
The clouds puff up like a ball of snow,
The sun sings to me,
The thing that makes nature special is the magic from your heart,
Trust your heart, it will lead you to the beauty of the world,
Believe you can imagine anything you want,
follow your heart and end with a song.
Follow the Monarch's flight and end with a song!

The Cardinal
by Alvina Do

Like a red messenger, the Cardinal looks around its surroundings.
A delicate shadow appears as the Cardinal flies across the sky.
Its chirps are like gentle bells in the distance.
One look at its shining tail will look like silk in the sky.
The Cardinal is as black as coal and as red as a raging fire.
Its eyes twinkle like the many stars in the sky.
Why must this beautiful vision come and go instead of stay forever?
The Cardinal is a piece of art.
Many see it as an animal, but I see it as a cherish to our world.
A proud and happy bird is the Cardinal.

Snowmen
by Conner Snavely

When the sun goes down
All the snowmen come to life
They play and play all night
Throw snowballs at each other
When the sun comes up
They go back to sleep
No one will know
Who really ever threw the snowball

Feel the Love
by Benjamin O'Konski

Mama's love
Kissity-kiss
My loving heart's
All a bliss
Lovity-love
Mama's kiss
Love is my magic
And my drug
I'm a tiny cutie-pie
And a little lovebug!

Flowers
by Claire Baldacci

Flowers are pretty
Smelly, colorful, and big
Beautiful flowers

He Gave Me
by Madison Isada Cruz

He gave me
A brother that is oh so cute
A brother that is so thoughtful and kind
A brother that can often whine, but makes me smile from time to time
He gave me
A dad that plays King Kong chasing me
A dad that sits to draw with me
A dad that will take the time to teach me
A dad that likes to comfort me
He gave me
A mom that is always there for me
A mom that is ready to give me hugs and kisses when I fall and scrape my knee
A mom who always cooks and cleans, but still has time to care for me
A mom that makes me giggle with a tickle of my toes, picks flowers,
and takes the time to talk with me
A mom who is such a wonderful friend to me
HE gave me ... the best family EVER!
All this HE gave to me–isn't GOD so GOOD!

Laughing
by Tabatha Green

Laughing
Happiness, joyful
Flattering, amusing, joking
Comedy, theatre, feelings, hurting
Embarrassing, weeping, pain, hiding
Hurtful, unhappiness
crying

Earth Day
by Morgan Erdley

Earth Day hooray
Earth Day is my birthday
Beautiful Earth Day

Timmy Tommy Tucker
by Eric Simon

Timmy Tommy Tucker was at bat.
He wanted to get his first hit of the year, but then he saw a bat.
"Strike one," yelled the ump.
Right after that he had to tinkle.
So when Timmy Tommy Tucker went to the bathroom
the pitcher noticed he had a wrinkle.
Then he threw the ball
"Ball one," yelled the ump.
The next pitch was way outside, but he swung anyway.
"Strike two," yelled the ump.
Last chances for Timmy Tommy Tucker to get one hit all year, then the pitch.
Timmy Tommy Tucker hit it long and deep
and it went father and farther and gone home run.
So Timmy Tommy Tucker got his first hit all year, which was a homer.

The Bear
by Jensen Petros

There once was a scary bear
Was bald, he had no hair
Went swimming for an apple
Astonished he found some Campbells
And now he is a hare

A Poem of Friends
by Kate Klima

Friends are great, friends are fun,
You will find joy, in everyone.
Friends are fun, friends are sweet,
I can't wait, until we meet.
Friends are sweet, friends are great,
I want to see my friends, oh I just can't wait.
On the beach, we like to wade,
We like to enjoy, what God has made.
I love my friends, they love me,
God loves us, my friends and me.

A Changing Day
by Kate Marie Anderson

The kids all sigh
As the rain pours down
Oh my oh my
Thunder booming in the town
Everyone wished
For the sun to come out
The rain won't be missed
Without a doubt
Somehow someway
Their request came true
Now outside they can play
As the sky turns bright blue

Up, Up
by Brooke Wilmes

Up, up here we go
Here I am sitting by Joe
And there he is eating ham
Hey! There is his friend Pam
She likes to Jam, Jam, Jam
All you hear is Bam, Bam, Bam
Pam has a pet lamb
Her lamb's name is Ram
Oh NO, down, down!
NO Joe don't jump to the ground
Joe don't eat that hog
OK what about this dog
Don't eat my dog, Job
I run and get my dog
Let's go home now Job, let's see Bob.

A Cold Winter's Night
by Jason Ozmon

Walking home
so cold, so snowy.
Got to my car
that was parked half way there
with fogging up windows.
Oh, dear! Oh ,dear!
Got to my house,
walked through the doors.
So warm, so cozy.
When I did,
I walked up the stairs,
brushed my teeth,
got into bed
for a cold winter's sleep
and snowflakes danced in my dreams!

Love Those Eggs!
by Andrew Stewart

One of my favorite things to cook,
Is a fried egg sandwich, take a look!
I see the egg in my pan,
It seems as if it's getting a tan!
I can't touch my pan because it's too hot,
You must always use caution, like it or not.
The egg smells so good, I can hardly wait,
To see it in a sandwich on my plate.
I hear the egg go sizzle and pop,
About then it is time to stop.
I taste the egg, tomatoes, cheese, and toast,
It tastes so delicious I want to boast!
Yes, my fried egg sandwich is the best,
Some might even say I'm obsessed.

Rollercoaster Friend
by Lauren Borchart

Like a rollercoaster, my friend now,
but not then.
We go up, we have fun.
We go down, not to speak anymore.
Around in loops.
Hold on, it's getting rough!
Then back up, I'm your best friend,
then your worst enemy.
But like a rollercoaster, our ride must end,
to a smooth stop.
My rollercoaster friend.

If You Want To Find Blue
by Dorothy Miller

If you want to find blue look at the sky
Look at a blue house or look at a blue paper.
If you want to find blue look at Play-Doh
Look at a blue pencil, blue blanket, a blue box or a blue book
Look at a blue wall, a blue jacket or a blue ball,
Look at a blue shirt, look at a blue flower
Look at a blue balloon or a blue toy
Look at a blue bear, look at a blue computer, look at a blue tote
To find blue, look at a blue water bottle.

My Brother
by Caroline Nham

Carter isn't just a brother
Carter camps he sleeps
he's a good brother to me
Carter shoots hoops
he even eats
fruit loops
I enjoy having him around
he is cheerful
he is loud
he can't settle down.
That's why
he is one of a kind

The Old Cold Man
by Lucky Bolden

There once was a man named clip
He fell in a ditch and broke his hip
He was old
He was cold
Then he had to board a ship.

Homework
by Nicholas Shivum Sooknanan

Homework can be a chore
Sometimes it can be so much more
Reviewing subjects taught in school
Being brilliant is so cool ...
Homework, homework it sings out
It sings out with a loud, loud shout.
In my backpack lays my book
There's my homework, take a look ...
Homework, what a lengthy task
Difficult questions thus ask
Problem-solving done with ease
Achievement our goal, we aim to please ...
Homework can be easy it can be hard
It can be tricky and make us mad
The bonus points we gain each day
Helps us excel in work and play ...
Homework terrible, homework good
Homework made us understood
Video games are loads more fun
But learning enhances when homework's done.

Turquoise
by Caroline Gnatowski

Turquoise is the color of the ocean
Turquoise is the water in the fish aquarium
Turquoise is the flowers in a garden
Turquoise is the beauty of the waves
Turquoise smells like salt water
Turquoise tastes like Gatorade
Turquoise sounds like a spring day
Turquoise looks like the beach skies
Turquoise feels like the breeze on a warm day
Turquoise makes me happy
Turquoise is my favorite color

Autism
by Brenna Leonard

Some people say,
That children with autism cannot play,
But they are still good friends to have around,
I always see them having a good time on the playground.
There are many autistic kids at my school,
And they are very cool.

Siblings
by Jaylen Delacruz

I hate siblings.
I hate them so much.
I'd rather go in a box with a fox.
All I hear is Waa! Waa!
All day.
I'd rather have a race in space
than have siblings.
And I just want to mention ...
that I don't get all the attention!

In the Hands of the Children
by Patrizia Manziano

The future adults, the next generation,
come on everybody it's earth's invitation.
Save every tree, choose well every choice
'cause you all are nature's personal voice.
Recycle the paper, don't forget to reuse,
take care of the animals and never abuse.
Help all the forests, jungles and rivers,
be not just receivers, but givers.
Speak for the lakes, the trees and the birds,
you say what they'd say if they had the words.
Help rebuild the cities that have suffered a pain,
all the work you do will never be in vain.
Think of the people that will come after you,
think a little while ... then take a walk in their shoes.
The whole world is waiting for your songs to be sung,
let the melody sound as brave as your soul.

America
by Genna Hebert

America, strong, brave, united
Nothing can frighten us
We are the melting pot of cultures
All of the wars we've fought
The rise and fall of the economy
Our tragedies
Our victories
When things get tough, we don't hide or quit
We face the facts, and find a solution
We had to earn our freedom,
Earn our land
Earn respect
We've been through so much
But we did it together
United as one, the United States of America
The home of the brave!

The Star
by Brandon Prem Sooknanan

Bright and glowing you are
Shining in the night from afar
Watching down on us from the sky
In the heavens way up high ...
There you are each night
When dusk covers light
You brighten the sky so all can see
Just how beautiful you can be ...
Twinkling bright in the night
Oh what a brilliant sight
Millions of sparkingly stars are seen
How did you come to be?????
Scattered everywhere in the sky
A shooting star sometimes flies by
A wish made, a moment in time
Dreams fulfilled without a sigh ...
Wondrous star how did you appear
I'm so glad you are here
You brighten the world with your precious light
When day starts turning into night ...

Fly
by Landon Javens

There was a fly
In the sky
With a cut in his eye
So he went outside
And took a big breath
Before his death
Then he yelled real loud
Up to a cloud
And as he began to fall
He sighed as he thought of all
His friends and family
And hoped that their days would be filled with glee.

Trees
by Max McKoy

Trees so tall
a mouse so small
Trees make oxygen for us all.

Cats
by Alex Dresdner

We are the cats, small but brave
don't stand in our way, our glare is grave
we don't have masters, we stand alone
when we get angry, our stare is stone.
when the day is gone and tonight is here
we wake and roam around, clear
that even at a dog's frightening bark
we cannot be scared; we can see in the dark
Luscious fur, delicate paws
we can do what we want; cats don't have laws
beautiful figures, we arch our spines in stretch
and we bound across the grass when there's a mouse to catch.
purrs and hisses, moans and yowls
you doubt we can talk but there are words in our meows
we are saying that even though ostriches are tall
cats are the most stunning creatures of all.

Cats
by Kassidy Mills

I have an orange cat
He is very fat
He sleeps on my bed
Sometimes on my head
His name is Sunshine
We have a fun time
I love him a lot
With all of his orange spots

In the Morning
by Payton Schlosser

in the morning
you will hear
a little
Red Bird chirping
it sings songs so
lovely
it moves it's little head
up
in the shadow
of the tree
in the morning.

Dogs
by Cameron Gray

Dogs
Cute, loveable
Fury, loud, fast
Huggable, loyal, ugly, mean,
Scary, slow, silent
Hairy, allergenic
Cats

Katie the Snowman
by Katherine Strongarone

My snowman's body is big and round.
I dress him just like me.
He's wearing my favorite hat and gloves
For everyone to see!

Stars
by Cora Sheppard

Stars are bright
Like a light
In the night
The stars are shinning
And they brighten
My night
The light is so bright
It lights up the night.
The shape is like gold
That is what I've been told
Some nights I can actually hold
What I've been told
Because the nights are just so gold.
Stars are like spirits
Dancing in the night
Saying, "Oh, look at me here."
Out there
They seem to stare
All through the night!

That's My Little Brother
by Madeline Michael

There he is as happy as can be,
Smiling, smiling that's all I can see.
Sitting by a tree looking at me.
When he shows his smile I love him so,
that I want to reach out and tickles his toes.

A Beautiful Day
by Cassondra Janssen

When the glowing of the moon
Goes down and the shining of
The sun comes up the light of
Day begins to blossom on the
Earth.
The sun feeds the flowers
With its beauty as they
Awaken while the birds chirp
And the dewdrops go away for
One more Day.
While the children play until
The end of the day the sun goes
Back to sleep and the moon again
Awakens, the day says goodnight
As the world starts sleeping.

The World Outside
by Eaden Javens

The world outside is one-of-a-kind
with the grass swaying,
and the crickets chirping.
The world outside is one-of-a-kind
with the sky so high,
and the birds singing.
The world outside is one-of-a-kind
Because each outside is different!

Summer
by Kaitlyn Kluck

Summer is blue and green
It tastes like lemonade.
It sounds like splashes in a pool.
It smells like campfires at night.
It looks like happy and playful children.
And feels like warm breezes.

Handball!
by Jessica Stewart

It's sportsmanship day for fifth graders,
And it is time to play handball.
As the sun is waking up on a Saturday,
Kids come from nine different schools,
To compete in a tournament.
When I'm on the sidelines,
I help pass the ball as fast as lightning.
When I play defense,
I am like a barrier that stops the ball
From getting into the goal.
When I play offense,
I help shoot the ball like a rocket
Into the opponent's goal.
After each game is over,
My team and I shake our opponents' hands,
And say, "Good game!" no matter who won.
There are smiles all around,
And that is what good sportsmanship is all about!

Wild
by Haleigh Theis

Wild
Mysterious, beautiful
Full of surprises
Animals hiding in shadows
Wild

Wolves
by Danielle Gish

Majestic, unique
Howling, running, jumping
Oh! their musical howls.
Magnificent wolves

Pink
by Julia Barron

Pink is the color of love.
Pink is when I blush.
Pink is usually girly.
Pink is red's best friend.
Pink smells like flowers.
Pink tastes like diamonds.
Pink sounds like a choir of birds.
Pink looks like a piggy bank.
Pink feels like cotton candy.
Pink makes me feel pretty.
Pink is the heart on Valentine's Day.

The Worst Plane Crash
by Jake Hogan

Once there was a plane crash.
The plane did 5 spins.
Then it lost it's motor and a wing.
Then it went straight down.
The driver pulled the grips.
They lost their GPS.
So when he saw an airport it really was a hill.

Autism
by Tracey Lam

Don't be scared,
Don't be mean,
They are still the same like you and me.
They want to be like you and me.
Then be a friend,
And introduce yourself.
And give a piece of friendship.
Open your heart and become a greater person.
Together we can help Autism.
Be a giver,
Not a hater,
Be nice, together we can make a brighter future.

Dakota
by Dakota Overman

D is for darling and cute
A is for awesome, cool as can be
K is for kindness, willing to share
O is for outstanding, which is so awesome
T is for timing, always on time
A is for angel, sweet as can be

Carlos
by Carlos Dominguez

C-is for cake eater.
A-is for caring about animals.
R-is for fast runner.
L-is for lucky.
O-is for organizer.
S-is for skateboarder.

Spring
by Megan Cordary

Spirits are high
Playing in the rain
Rising sun
Incredible
Never fear spring is here
Giving rainbows here and there

Animals
by Tiffany Dinh

Animals are friendly
Never let you down
Is always energetic
Merry all the time
Always will be your best friend
Loving
So fun to play with

Football
by Jose Benavides

Fun
Outlandish
Outstanding
Terrific
Best sport ever
Amazing
Limitless
Lively

Legos
by Cale Bickler

Links together
Everything imaginable
Going to build forever
Outstanding colors
Steady work

Barkley
by Tyler Koslucher

Barks a lot
Annoying sometimes
Runs a lot
King of dogs
Loving pet
Everyone thinks he is cute
You would love him too

ABCs of Living In a Small Town
by Isaac Habedank

Around me I see people who
Become
Community,
Differences
Erased,
Forming friendships
Goodbye to strangers
Hello friends!

Man!
by Parker Tjaden

Macho!
Awesome!
Nailed it!

Isaac
by Devin Holte

Isaac is the best at football
Send the ball down the field
Allow him to get by you and he will be gone
Amazing
Catch! Touchdown!

Kaleb
by Brekken Mattson

Kaleb is a lot of fun
Also he is my brother
Looks like me
Everybody I know likes him
But he is really smart

All About Me
by Olivia Ware

O is for overly nice.
L is for loving and kind.
I is for intelligent
V is for very helpful.
I is for independent.
A is for asking and curious.

Amber
by Samara Verhel

Amber is my training horse
My best friend forever
Beside me all the time
Every day I see her I get so excited
Riding off at the end of the day

Kennison Amill

The Ocean
by Kennison Amill

The sun sets golden pink.
I sit so far from the city lights twinkling faintly on the horizon.
The glossy water ripples as I touch it.
The moon's reflection glides over the stillness.
A cool breeze makes me shiver.
From above,
the water looks frozen,
but I know another world is alive underneath.

2nd Place

Chelsie Barrientos

A Total Destruction of the Heart
by Chelsie Barrientos

When your parents die, it feels like someone you loved
just decided to pick up and abandon you.
At first, I denied it. I put up walls, sealing myself from the outside world,
and soon, it became a distant memory.
Eventually, I found myself making "deadlines" to when I would feel better.
When the time came around, I would pretend to feel better,
when inside, I knew otherwise.
Now, all I had left was my sister.
Together, we maintained the faintest trace
of hope that we would pull through.
I felt like I had to comfort all of my parent's grieving friends,
and there was no time for me to grieve.
One month later, my sister passed away,
right when the feeling of loneliness in my stomach was fading away.
I was jealous that she could just drop off the map when times got tough,
and I was left to pick up the pieces.
I felt like my family was unraveling faster than a ball of yarn,
and everyone around me was dying.
As I walked home on that dreary, rainy day,
I decided that there must have been a greater reason why
I was the only one in my family left,
and I felt like I was on the verge of discovering it ...

1st
Place

Lilly Era

For as long as she can remember,
Lilly has wanted to be an author,
and in fact, competed in a recent school poetry jam
in which she took top honors.
An entertainer at heart,
she also aspires to be a singer, artist, and actress,
and has appeared in a number of dance performances.
She credits her brother, who is also an author,
for inspiring her to write.

The Lilac
by Lilly Era

A Lilac blooms by the clearest lake
it sparkles in the sun
A purple so delicate
it looks as if it would shatter like glass at the slightest touch
from this Lilac a whisper seems to come
like the faintest,
quaintest,
angelic hum.
It never ceases,
never stops.
And in the spring mornings,
come the sparkling dewdrops
like nothing in this world the drops reflect
and bend the world around them
but yet, through this dewdrop,
everything blurs
in a magic with remarkable power.
A Lilac blooms by the clearest lake
it sparkles in the sun.

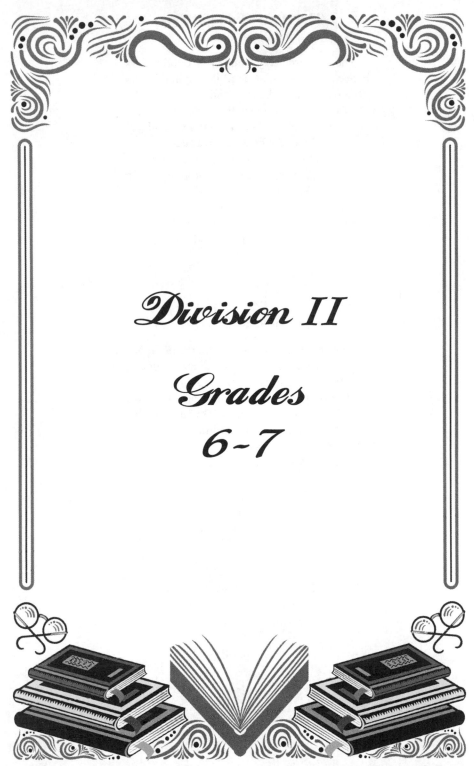

Division II

Grades 6-7

The Dark Midnight Skies
by Annie Choudhry

The sky turns gray while the ground is dark.
Someone is around me while I'm in this park.
The owls start to hoot … and hoot … and hoot.
I'm lonely and I hear the ocean water go–
Whoosh … whoosh … and whoosh.
I will not be eaten by a shark.
I'm alone with no one, no one around–
And I want to cry but no one's going to see me–
Accept for the midnight sky.
This is crazy.
Where am I?
It's time to go … and go,
Bye bye!

The Hunt
by Vera Thomas

Lurking in the distance a lion creeps about,
watching his prey without any doubt.
He's ready to pounce, any second now,
Then out comes a roar with a big ol' growl.
Chasing and leaping, over big and small,
Nothing in his way, nothing's too tall.
Finally he jumps and squeaks in the air,
he's a little kitten, nothing but a mouse to scare.

Day and Night
by Allie Styron

Day
Hot, Sunny
Playing, Swimming, Running
Friends, Family, Love, Life
Sleeping, Talking, Relaxing
Cold, Dark
Night

Through the Years
by Brian Cheng

What I've seen behind the lines
Is something everyone has seen, dating at twelve
Or friends losing themselves
Where have those old friends gone?
Lost forever in the Sands of Time?
Or lost to the mysterious ways of the sublime?
People won't take the time to see what they're leaving behind
Instead, they join the ranks of the teenaged kind
Breaking their binds they leave friends behind
Becoming arrogant they tell you to leave
You find it hard to believe
You sink and observe
And think of the friendship you could have conserved
You think of the years gone by
You know it's time to say goodbye
As they leave you to the dust
And you fade into the dusk

The Apprehensive Soul
by Jack Schefer

He approaches the forest
Entering the horrific grasp of fear
A moonbeam strikes the eyes of many
Awaiting the apprehensive soul
He enters the darkness
An unmistakable blanket of solitude overtakes him
He sees the glint of on looking eyes
Awaiting the apprehensive soul
He pulls his dagger
Light engulfs the resentful clearing
All foul demons scatter except one who stands
Awaiting the apprehensive soul
The single demon retreats to the darkness
And reappears brandishing a black scythe
Weapons ready he engages the demon who is
Awaiting the apprehensive soul
A single stab
The demon was bested
For no longer shall the foul demons be
Awaiting the apprehensive soul

Summer Fun
by Jordan Jenkins

In the summer time,
on a hot day.
playing on a beach,
next to the bay
Having lots of fun,
outside by the sun
swimming in the pool,
with water that is cool,
on a break from school.

Colleges
by Brandon Groenewold

Duke (NC)
Swimming - Men finish 3-6 and women finish 6-5
Michigan (MI)
Football - finished 7th in their conference
Texas (TX)
Football - last in their conference
TCU (TX)
Football - #1 in their conference
Pittsburgh (PA)
Basketball (My friend's favorite college team)
Iowa (IA)
Basketball - they have a record of only 3-12
Kansas (KA)
Basketball - they are #2
Notre Dame (PA)
Lacrosse - #6
SMSU (MN)
Baseball - I know Drew Benson who hit a 400 ft. home run,
also the guy I call Drew Brees
DUKE
The college I am going to

Never Again
by Kris Crickenberger

You see what you want.
You head for it,
but all in one moment
your blinded
like if you were staring at the sun.
You realize it's the fuzz.
The rain pitter patters as it hits your footsteps.
But your caught.
Next, you find yourself in a suit and tie.
After three months in a cell.
Video and finger prints laugh
as you fight for your life.
But you lose.
You find out that you will never see your wife again
or the three month old girl
never again.
I would know.
It happened to me.

Spring
by Irene Franco

I like spring
Spring, spring
Trees are growing and blossoming
Spring, spring
Birds are singing
Spring, spring
Lots of shopping
Spring, spring
Lots of bright colors
Spring, spring
That's why I like spring
Spring, spring

What Will You Do?
by Sophie Warrick

Dolphins–like angels in the water.
Dolphin captivity–lonely stages to a painful death.
Captive dolphins helpless and miserable.
Successful dolphins that survive a violent capture,
Suffer
An overwhelming death within 90 lonely days.
Harassed dolphins,
Round and round and round
Swim in small circles,
Committing a frustrating suicide every day.
Trainers supply desperate dolphins dead fish,
while the free and joyful dolphins happily hunt.
Many killed because of
Horrible capture shock,
Chlorine poisoning, and stress related illnesses.
What will you do?

Angelica's Feelings
by Angelica Allery

Crooked minded,
don't know where to start having my own style,
but everywhere I look it's cloudy.
Have my own ways: sitting on the floor because I'm mad,
looking at myself in the mirror…it makes me mad.
So many things so little time. I think I know why I wrote this poem.
Well my poem doesn't really rhyme but now I can let my feelings go.

Frogs
by Vanessa Thompson

Frogs are bouncing high
Leaping today, tonight, always
On the water shadows leap
Summer is her jump for joy
Bright and shiny fast they are

Hunting
by Tommy Lagunas

The dog wags her tail
The dog is ready to hunt
Time to find pheasants

Love and Passion
by Alyssa Hogan

Like honey, love leaves a joyous taste in your mouth.
It smells like a flower in full bloom.
It feels warm like as the sun and as soft as a blanket.
Love sounds like jazz music, slowly, rocking you to sleep.
It looks as beautiful as a sunset.
Love and passion have so many feelings you can never stop at one definition

No! Don't Go In There!
by Andreá Braxton

No! Don't go in there!
Have you lost your head?
There are spiders and witches,
cobwebs too!
Oh go ahead, you hard-headed fool.
Go ahead, you little rascal you!
Just watch as your heamps
like a kangaroo!
It won't be long before you—BAM!
Did you hear that tat-tat
on the wall?
Hurry up and leave,
before they get you all!
They'll come for you like moths to light!
Hurry, run with all your might!
Finally we are out of there!
Oh, but wait.
Hear that scary tune?
I see a witch!
Eyes glisten like a silver spoon.
Oh no! She's coming, oh—POOF
Oh, well I guess I'll see you soon.

The Loving Dreams
by Maya Elliott

In the hazy dawn of every morning,
within my thoughts comes a new light
of loving memories and visions of the
the years before me. The happiest
wonders are in my thoughts when I sleep
away from the tragedy and internal war of life
and hope. As I lie awake at night, I know now
that there is no way to get away from it all except
in the dreams of a loving soul.

Winter Snow
by Cecilio Ramos

Across the snowy hills
Against the windy chills
Around a white fence
Outside it's so intense
During the rest of the day
Over the snow I play
Before I go
Down to lick the snow
Up I go home

A Letter To a Tree
by Jean-Luc Genereau

Dear Tree,
I'm sorry that you lose all your beautiful leaves in fall
and that you are blown over in storms.
I regret that you are chopped up for firewood like a butcher would chop up a ham.
I apologize that you are made into boards and wood chips
and that woodpeckers drill into you and that ants make their homes in you.
I want to thank you for creating oxygen because if you didn't we would all be dead.
I am also really angry at you because you supply paper that makes me do homework.
It's too bad that the people who plant you
can't keep up with the amount of trees cut down each year.
You might even go extinct!
I feel really ashamed for asking this, but will you please help me heat my house?
Sincerely,
Jean-Luc Pierre Genereau

Peace Parade
by Jojo Orbeck

One day I know it will all change,
You can be you and not be strange.
One day we'll all march in a peace parade.
People all different, sizes and age.
One day I know you'll love me for me,
For there's always something beyond what you see.
One day we'll all march in a peace parade.
I know who I am and who I ought to be.
One day I know we'll all march with each other.
We might even learn to love one another.
One day we will all march in a peace parade.
God made us all equal; sisters and brothers.

Clouds
by Daniel Coakley

Clouds are big and white
floating over us all day long.
They make snow and rain.

Storms In the Morning
by Jacob Stephani

Early in the morning.
Dew moistened grass lay lifeless on the ground.
Blooming flowers relax and drink.
Singing birds chirp in the misty air.
Skies are gray.
Calm winds stir the fallen leaves.
Broken gutters knock against the house.
Baseball gloves are rapidly gathered.
Plop! Plop!
Animals scurry to their shelters.
Ditches change into raging rivers.
Lawn lakes form in seconds.
It's done.
Animals come out from hiding.
Children play in yard puddles
A cleansed world has awoken.

The Patriot
by Christopher Fly

A young stripling warrior with a musket set on his shoulder,
readies across the battlefield to fight an army thick as a boulder.
He seeks to attain vengeance for his loving wife Ann,
while the redcoats watch and say he is not even a man.
With a fighting spirit and a Star Spangled Banner o'er his head,
he charges strongly and is blown down with a curtain of lead.
The young soldier couldn't walk but still fought along his brothers,
he had made up his mind he wouldn't end up like the others.
The young soldier was hit in the chest by a fragment of a bullet,
he had been shot down and nobody even knew it.
While the young boy was down he said with his dying breath,
"Nothing will stop this fight for liberty whether it be hell or a gruesome death."
The velvet red blood of the young soldier coated the battlefield,
yet the rest of the army continued fighting and wouldn't yield.
Some people say this story isn't true but don't believe that just yet,
because if you listen hard enough you can hear the cry of the young patriot.

Love
by Hakeem Peterson

Love, you make people feel good inside.
People say "you don't last forever."
I say "you make it last forever unless your love is for real."
People say "you make us nervous and scared to say to our lover."
I say "say what you what to say her or him."
Love, you will last forever because our love is for real.

Spring
by Seth Miller

Spring, the snow is gone
The fish begin to spawn
April showers bring May flowers
Pollen is in the air and it's time to make memories
Watch flowers bloom
So you can watch the bees and robins come back
with the monarchs and all other creatures
Love is in the air.

Peaster Bunny
by Shreoshee Barua

I have once seen an amazing animal
I am not sure if it's a reptile or a mammal
I told my parents about what I saw
But they didn't believe me at all
I am not sure what this animal is called
But it was incredibly tall
I just named it whatever came to my mind
I called it Peaster bunny because the name seem to rhyme
Oh beautiful Peaster bunny
How cute and cuddly you are
You have peas in your ears and you have peas in your fur
You can hop on your legs
You can twirl on your toes
You dance until peas come out of your nose!
You are a weird creature but to me you are very sweet
Though no one believes me,
I will surely remember to take a picture next week!

Pteranodon
by Olivia Gaffney

What's that flying in the sky?
It's a Pteranodon flying so high.
It's swooping it's soaring into the ocean
quickly coming back with a mouthful of fish,
it's munching it's crunching
for Brunch or maybe for Lunch?
He sleeps in a nest for a good night sleep.
You may wonder how do they fly so high?
They have hollow bones, which make them light
so they can fly in the sky.
When predators try to eat them
they go up, up they go.
They fly threw the sky to a safe place to eat.
If I could have a dinosaur
I would pick this flying pet.

Spring Walk
by Aaron Seyer

Cruising down the sidewalk
It's all so cool
When I started whistling
The birds started whistling too
It's all quiet
Till I stopped
Because I found a penny
It pays to walk

Backpack
by AJ Quade

My backpack follows me everywhere,
When I set it down and turn around it hops up off the ground.
When ever I look back it jumps behind a chair, its giving me quite a scare.
Like a thief in the night it is never in sight.
Though when I get out of bed it lays there dead.

The Path
by Megan Greene

I walk along the jagged path
With the birds singing in the trees,
and the stream lightly cooing.
A bumblebee flies past me as yellow as the sun.
The leaves dance high in the trees,
and I sigh solemnly as I walk away.

Rotted Meatloaf
by Monica Morin

Meatloaf Meatloaf
Icky, icky, goo
Messy, messy, messy
Iew, iew, iew
Dark brown rust
With a little blue
Hopefully no one likes it
Not even you!

Your House
by Julian Castro

How big is your house
Is it as small as a spouse
What if it became a mansion
With a really big expansion
Would it have lights
With lots of knights
Or maybe a door
With some tiled floor
Maybe if you have the money
You could even buy some honey
And that's not all
I will surprise you with a ball
Having a house is all that matters
But it might all just shatter

Basketball
by Claudia Hernandez

Basketball is fun
I'm dribbling down the court
My team is the best

School
by Karl Palenkas

Some think school is cool,
some think school is tight.
Some think teachers drool,
some think school's just not right.
School is important,
to get a good career.
Some are more hesitant,
and just stay away in fear.
School is needed,
In order to survive these times.
Once you have succeeded,
You've got more than dimes.
School is sometimes fun,
All from preschool to college.
Once you have your college diploma,
Your school experience is done.

Losing Someone You Love
by Destiny Massey

Losing someone you love is like a storm.
Comes and drifts you away.
Scared and alone in the darkness,
don't even know how much you can weigh.
The cost of losing someone you love is hard.
It's so emotional it feels like you got hit with a punching card.
The tears are gone but the pain inside is still there.
Losing the only person you had, there's no spare.
You pray for them to come back,
resume where you left off, play the track.
But unfortunately, you can't do anything,
you feel like a sack.
Maybe, just maybe, you will see them again
but now keep that smile.

Never Say Never
by Arun Bhattasali

Walking with Mother Nature touched my heart,
wherever I was, the spirit never fell apart.
Plants and animals filled the land,
the beautiful scenery, never bland.
Ripples of water in numberless streams,
this kind of life, only in dreams.
I was stranded, on that one distant cay,
I knew no one would come to save the day.
Even though it was the worst of times,
I knew I would never lose them rhymes.
Pacing back and forth along the beach,
waiting for a brave rescuer to reach.
The flame lit, with a beckoning glow,
the fire within me was about to show.
I wasn't going to give up the fight,
I worked hard, and used much of my might.
Then one day when I heard an eerie sound,
it was a plane that had finally come around.
The pilot came and asked me, "What's Up!"
I replied, "This is what happens when I don't give up!"

My Brother
by Maria Leondaridis

People ask me sometimes:
Do you hate your brother for being mean to you?
I say to them not all sure I get mad at him, but
We're siblings that fight, it's what we do.
If you ask why I love my bro here are some reasons.
I love him because he is part of my family
Though he makes fun of me
Though he is mean to me
I love him anyway.
Because when my parents and grandparents die
All we have is each other
Though this poem may not rhyme
I hope it touches your heart just like mine
Cause this comes from my feelings
I do love my big brother
That is not a lie

Random
by Alexandra Morris

Turn songs up when you want to
The winter is made through you while you sing
Stories help write songs
Understand together you and your mom can make stories to make songs
Think about the stars
It is nice
Who tells you funny things
Pumpkin
When old pigs walk with you, you can make a wish
No one should cry in the summer
Don't worry be happy
Slow, soft, silly sounds while I'm wishing on a star
The world is in your midst
But it has only just begun
Birds chirp
Dogs bark
All these sounds are a perfect harmony
Purple Irises sway in the breeze
Sun shines
Spring is on the way

Life As I Know It
by Jenna Acheson

I try
I want to make people believe I'm someone I'm not
I feel insecure
If you really knew how I felt inside you wouldn't blame me
Why do you stare, laugh, or groan?
I sit silently knowing life as I know it is a giant sinkhole
Everyone I know and love is disappearing
Like the sun setting, and the moon rising
But does the sun really ever leave?
It's kind of like the people I love
They walk out the door but they will always remain in my heart
Why does it happen?
Well why should I know?
Even if I did is it any of your business?
So this right here is my free verse
Like it or not. I really don't care.
My emotions lie on this piece of paper in front of you.
I trust that you don't laugh or giggle
I love everything about this piece of paper
Or do I?

Favorite Place
by Alyssa Stratton

The lake
On a warm and sunny summer day
All day
Morning doves hooting,
People's bobbers going kerplunk,
Boats cruising by
Lots of people swimming,
Little paddle boats,
People in big boats
I go swimming,
I go on boat rides,
Playing in the yard,
Eating lunch
In the summer
Super happy

Spring
by Billy Coburn

The leaves on the trees
Are as green as the grass.
The sun is shining high
As the plants are growing bigger
As the bees collect their nectar,
The butterflies shine with their beautifulness.
The whistle of the wind makes me want to say
Spring is here!

Beautiful
by Alyssa Landford

Beautiful is ... a red and blue flower blooming in the Spring.
Beautiful is ... a woman dressed in a lovely dress.
Beautiful is ... a forest filled with trees and flowers.
Beautiful is ... just being yourself.

A Candy
by Brooke Chesley

Pigmented and extravagant flavors
Chewing and sucking
Noisily
Jolly Rancher

My Perfect Pictures
by Kristen Fredericks

I am a kitten, prancing at all the ants that crawl
I am a bumblebee buzzing around the tulips, daisies, and roses that smell so sweet
I am the black and white jersey that I wear to beat my opponents
I am the trick candles that get blown out every November fourth
I am the pouring down rain making gigantic puddles that cars splash through
I am a dog getting walked by my owner on an exquisite day
I am the gusts of wind that blow against unique and friendly faces
I am the mighty eagle soaring high in the impeccable azure sky
I am the blanket that I wrap up in every morning,
when I join my mom outside to listen to the birds.

The Game
by Casey Wrabley

Driving in the mountains up and around
in the middle of nowhere, nothing to be found
all of the sudden a quaint little town.
Car after car as far as the eye can see
thousands of smiling faces
what a fantastic party
Moving along through the sea of fans
all around the sound of the marching band
the sea comes alive as the players arrive
Orange and maroon, squished, so many people, no room
the crowd begins to roar as the F-18s soar
the music starts thumping, everyone START JUMPING!
The ball is kicked everyone begins to run
the battle has now begun
as the ball moves from side to side, we hear the players collide
The game nears the end, the score is tied
but we drive down the field one more time
catching the ball, he dives across the line
Time is up, the crowd erupts
the game is done the Hokies have won!

Colors
by Steven Thomas

Colors are red
Colors are blue
Colors are yellow
That shines over our head
There are many colors in the rainbow.

A Guy From Maine
by Alec Rossi

There once was a person from Maine.
Who had finally moved from Spain.
He had to unpack dirty socks
from a misshapen box.
Then realized that he left his toy train.

Mudslide Football
by David Rios

The ball flies through the air
People diving into each other
You hear them bark orders
Blue 42, set, set, hike
People getting hit, touchdown, and the crowd goes wild
Halftime to rest from all that work
Now it's time to go on the field
And they are so mad they make mud stripes on their faces
And they said blue fifty, set, set, hike
They go down into the mud
4th quarter
It's 14 – 14
There's only 5 minutes on the clock
They said hike, the ball went flying into the air
He catches it and slides in the mud into the touchdown

Why Me?
by Ayzia (Asia) Bumbrey

Why am I here Lord? Why am I breathing?
Why am I black?
He doesn't know and I don't know either.
I call out aloud WHY ME!!? Nobody answers me.
Am I invisible or something?
I see a kid I say "Hey you kid come here!"
The kid runs.
I see a man I say "Hey you man come here!"
He scurries.
I guess I'm just a voice ready to be seen.

Love
by Vanessa Vuolo

Love lives with us through thick and thin.
It lies in our hearts within.
For that special someone who will be there first.
For someone who will come in with a "BURST"!!!
But for me love did not stay too long.
For I know now that love is nothing but a song.
Your bitterness has struck me like a dart.
But somehow you always find a place in my heart.

Softball Chick
by Amber Jackson

I am a softball chick
I wonder if I'll make Rage
I hear Shannon Parrlett!
I see my ball fly
I want a grand slam
I am a softball chick
I pretend I am Jenny Finch
I feel the ball going into my glove at first
I touch the runner
I worry about striking out
I cry when we lost and got second in All Stars
I am a softball chick
I understand when we lose
I say the best cheers ever
I dream to be on TV
I try my best and more
I hope we go to state
I am a softball chick

Come Home
by Megan Horsley

Come home so I can feel you pull my covers up at night.
Come home to feel my warm hand in yours crossing the street.
I know you're doing what's right, but I still need you. Come home.
Come home to see me dance to my favorite songs.
Come home for me to run to when my heartbreaks and your tears roll.
I know you got to fight, but I still miss you.
Come home.
Come home to see me take my team to state.
Come home so I can look in the stands and see your face.
They say you're gone, I won't say goodbye. Come home.
Come home to meet the man of my dreams.
Come home so I can walk down the aisle with you.
I'm still your little girl, come home to me. Come home.
Come home to see your new grandbaby.
Come home so I can tell you stories. Are you still there? Come home.
Come home to watch them walk across that stage, a child no more.
Come home to wipe my tears when they leave.
I guess you really are home, wait for me to
Come home.

Sentinel of the Forest
by Ciera Carlund

The beautiful brown bark,
From the branches to the roots,
It sways in the wind as if it was dancing to a tune,
A home for little creatures,
Long, Thick, Short, Thin,
Leaves, No Leaves, Flowers, or not,
No two are quite the same.

Shadow
by Jaquel Whitehead

Shadow you follow me everywhere even when it's as dark as night.
You follow me when I can't see you.
You follow me during those hot summer days.
But shadow I do have one question for you.
Why can you see me but I don't seem to always see you?
Well I guess that's the meaning of being a shadow.

Moving
by Kayli Ginocchio

Toys in boxes on the floor
Books in boxes in the rooms
Clothes on hangers on the beds
Grandparents crying in the doorway
Furniture under tarps in the living room
Eating off of paper plates is boring
Crazy kids running around making Mom mad
Tired parents packing boxes all through the night
Huge moving truck in the street with tons of men
Finally packed everything in the truck
One last check throughout the house in all the rooms
Saying goodbye to my parents is the hardest
Watching Mom and Dad go with the truck behind
Ten days at Grandparents' house was awesome
Time to go to our new house Minnesota
Saying goodbye to my grandparents and uncle was hard
Settling in was very fun while running around

Karl
by Mac Greeman

In 2010 my uncle died
As that happened a crow flied
His kids left so sad
While I sit there scared and mad
I just know he's in a happier place
I wish I could see his face.

Softball
by Meghan Thompson

A sport some people love
Other people despise it
A bat, ball, glove, and helmet
Are my most prized valuables
I see the diamond as a second home
Enough dirt to cover a mansion
The narrow, long dugout
Where players scream out cheers
Home plate calls your name
The ball screaming as the pitcher releases it
Coming off the bat at 100 miles per hour
Running around the bases, screeching to a halt
Teammates going wild
I can't wait until the next game

Little Ghost Shrimp
by Johnathan Wall

I am a little ghost shrimp that lives beneath the sea.
Nobody can see me.
Poor me, poor me.
I tried to party with Miss Tuna.
She thinks that she is a barracuda,
but really she is the chicken of the sea.
Miss Tuna can't see me.
Poor me, poor me.
I don't know why she can't see me.
Maybe one day Miss. Tuna can see me
I guess I'll go back to my little coral
at the bottom of the sea.
Poor me, poor me.

Forever and a Day
by Bridgette Helms

Your blue eyes,
your great smile,
give me butterflies
that last awhile.
To know you're all mine,
it makes me feel fine.
I shed a tear
to know its been almost a year.
You're who I'll adore
and love forever more.
You've been by my side
through thin and wide.
April two thousand ten
is how long its been.
You've dealt with all this
there's nothing more to miss.
If I didn't have you,
oh what would I do?
Forever and a day,
hope it stays this way!

I Am a Raindrop
by Danielle McAlister

I am a raindrop,
Cool and wet.
Falling down, down, down
Right to the ground
In puddles, creeks, and rivers.
I am so little yet so powerful,
I cause flooding,
And tears from many people.
People don't notice but, I cry too.
I don't want to ruin their homes,
Or take their loved ones.
Just so many of me
Can cause such tragic damage.
I am a raindrop.

Heartache
by Michelle Hundley

Trying to move on..
But, I can't help to think about you.
Everything I do...
Always reminds me of who you used to be.
My friends are tired of hearing your name.
But, they never think what its like to live with this pain.
Hearing words you never thought you would hear.
Vain words spilling out of your mouth..
Oh so clear.
I see you almost everyday.
Sometimes I see your face.
Sometimes you're turned away.
But, it makes me miss you even more either way?
You say you don't care anymore.
That's nice, because you already walked out the door.
My eyes aren't red, neither are they sore.
Because, when you left...
My tears all fell to the floor.

The Dark Fox
by Dane Luckman

I am as dark as the night
The undiscovered forest creaks
I stalk my prey as it veers close
Closer and closer it comes to death
I am debilitated
Wondering of my family
Remorseful for myself as I get lonely
When another needle sharp twig jabs my paw
I am pristine as the lunar light
Hungering for food I will not eat
I cry out in pain and agony
As I finally understand I'm dying
I long for my family
Although I know why we were separated
As I speak in my mother's soothing voice
I. Am. Lonely.

Rain
by Myrakle Thomas

Gloomy is the day
Falling from the clouds above
Pitter, patter, pain.

Would You If You Could, You
by Zoe Le Menestrel

What if you could,
Just diminish the sadness?
Extinguish the gloom, like a faintly flickering fire.
Erase the sadness of souls; killers, and liars.
Troubled.
Too much so.
Carrying a weight around so your feet drag into the ground.
Too burdened.
You may be innocent, by all means. To human beings?
Does it really matter to them?
I think not. Wallowing in their own self-containacy.
So would you if you could,
You. Would you take the burden of someone else's pain?
If even for a moment.
Hope is what you need. To overcome the darkness. The very hopeless monster.
Hope is the light to crush the crushing sadness.
So would you if you could?
Would you take the sadness, of someone else?
Would you if you could,
You.

Colors Splashing
by Thanh Nguyen

Blue, red, purple, green
These are the colors that I've seen
Birds chirping
Kids shouting
These are the sounds that I hear
Grass glittering
Splattered with water
Beautiful flowers
Butterflies fly
These are the special things
That remind me of spring!

Music
by Eva Boncich

I hear it when I'm lazy
I hear it when I go to sleep
Even my friend Daisy
Loves to hear the beat
Music is like art
So many different types
Sad ones
And happy ones
That everyone likes
Music is like waves in my ears
It mesmerizes me and my imagination
Music dancing in my ears
It's like a whole different sensation
Beep, Bop, Bap
Hear me clap
The words in my head
Do you like my rap?

Love
by Annastazia Lake

Love is a wonderful thing
It can make your heart rejoice and sing
Love is like a trophy you treasure it always
It is the special feeling you get when someone you like walks by you in the hallways
Love can sometimes send shivers down your spine
And make you wish things like I hope he is mine
Love can make you smile
Sometimes love only lasts a little while
It leaves you broken-hearted
You learn that your learning to love has only started
You will find that you will find someone new
And before you knew it your love for them grew
Then before you know it wedding bells have chimed
Now your wish has come true, you can finally call him mine
Now and then love passes, you feel lonely and depressed
You decide to give love a rest
But when you see the bride and groom dance
You decide to give love another chance

A Day Beneath the Waves
by Mark Stanley

I want to be
Under the deep blue sea
In a hidden cave far below the surface
Resting all day with my head
Laying down on the seabed
Watching the colorful fish race by
Like the bullets of the ocean
Go for a swim
How wonderful it's been
To feel the warm, silky water
Against my skin
When the day is done
And nightfall comes upon
I move back up to the freezing air
My memories from my perfect hideaway
Remember where it is
Come back one day I may
To spend another day
Beneath the deep blue sea.

The Ocean's Warning
by Megan Hoff

The lighthouse has burned out
now my ship is lost at sea
The rocks lay waiting beneath
the oars
for the death of me
Tumbling through troubled waters
drowning in a pool of salty tears
I let myself sink listlessly
Unafraid of my biggest fear
Death has been encountered
again and again on this unforgiving shore
where surviving is a battle
and living is a war
So always sail carefully
when upon the ocean blue
for if you are not wary
That could be the end of you.

Fly Away
by Megan Brobst

I met you when we were young,
Just in Pre-school
It was friendship at first sight
Together we were "cool"
I cried and played and laughed with you
We thought it'd never end
We squealed and hid when we watched "The Grinch"
So much time with you I spent
Fly, fly, fly away
Fly away my friend,
I love you no matter what,
Our friendship, I hope to mend
It was Mother's Day when I heard the news,
I couldn't help but cry
"She's moving out to California"
I couldn't believe my eyes
Someday, somehow we'll meet again
And find our friendship renewed,
But just for now, like I said,
I will always love you

Things That Are Gross ...
by Adrianna Wichmann

Snakes, they slither sneakily
My brother, he doesn't wash his hands
Shrimp, they're little and pink
Outside bathrooms, they never get cleaned
Lightning strikes, it could ZAP you!
Other people vomiting, I vomit
Hobos, they steal your money
Bugs, they stink!
Homework, I get too much!
Mud, it's watered down dirt
Snails, they're slimy!
Sardines, they're too fishy!
Books, they take too long
THESE THINGS ARE VERY GROSS!

Outside of Nature
by Jordan Rivers

Moss; absorbing the gray prey under its frightful leaves
Limes; a citrus fruit so sour, but sweet
Trees swaying to the songs of the wind
Praying Mantis; stalking the gardeners ... waiting to spring
Mint; lining up in rows, waiting to pounce
Pears; falling like a comet to the ground
Garden; protected by small and colorful elves
Envy; the hideous, green monster that shows our true selves

The Eyes of a Stranger
by Victoria Meilhammer

Some people look at me with eyes of wonder,
Some people look at me with eyes of pain,
Some see the difficulty and understand;
Some look down upon me to make themselves feel better,
but honestly I feel sorry for them.
Sorry that they don't see that we are all the same,
We all have feelings and we all need love.
So no matter who you are or what you look like know that you are always loved!

The Abyss
by Derek Sykes

In a wide, open abyss.
Down this far you take no risks,
But you wonder: Is something amiss?
This blue, seemingly never ending space.
You see lights that look like stars, performing a little Light Show.
In the sunless Blue, they are your source of light.
You are in an alien world, with no trace of sun.
Even farther down, it is almost Black now.
Silence, they say it is a virtue,
But down here, it terrifies you.
Your spine shivers, the silence screams at you.
No life this deep, yet you keep going.
The pressure is unimaginable.
You cannot take much more of this frightening Abyss.

I Miss You! - For My Pop-Pop (1917-2011)
by Jonelle Brown

Fly-Fly little birdie, you've shown us your love
Fly-Fly little birdie, Heaven awaits you above
You've shown us you care
Every which kind of way,
You'll always be there
Shining in the sun's rays.
Fly-Fly little birdie, you've shown us your love
Fly-Fly little birdie, Heaven awaits you above
You've shown us compassion
When we were all down,
You put your smile in action
And our hearts left the ground.
Fly-Fly little birdie, you've shown us your love
Fly-Fly little birdie, Heaven awaits you above
You've shown us good times
Every day of the year,
Your heart's still in mine,
Your spirit's still here.
Fly-fly little birdie, fly up to the sky,
Fly-fly little birdie, I'll see you next time.
~ Dedicated To James E. Fisher (my PopPop) ~ 1917-2011

What I See
by Kiley Weeks

Gnarled like a finger is the tree
Dead and knobbly, directly across from me
Home to grubs and insects is the log dry as the bones of a long dead dog
Tender like a mother's words are the shoots
Spread across the ground near my fuzzy brown boots
Loud and repetitive is the call of a teakettle bird in the trees so tall
Whispering gently is the soft spring breeze
Laughing as it rustles the leaves of the trees
Buzzing like man with news is a fly
Humming and strumming as it zips by
Bright is the sun by a pale white cloud
And you can feel from its presence that the sun is proud
I can hear the noises of the street
And of drivers shouting things that I won't repeat
I can see the drivers on the road, but they can't see me
But I don't mind because I'm in here in the forest where I want to be

Summer
by Sam Johnson

Summer hops in
With soccer and
Swimming in the pool
On a hot sunny day
With kids playing at the beach
Summer hops in

Lucy
by Abe Kummer

Her name was Lucy Johnson
Her skin was freckled and fair
She was extraordinarily smart
And she had flowing brunette hair
But she didn't know I existed
Or that my love for her burned so hot
Like one million thousand suns
But I didn't have a shot
One day she got very sick
Doctors said she was good as dead
The news hit me like a truck
And I got an ache inside my head
Then I went to see Death
For I couldn't let her die,
I asked if he'd bargain
And instead of her, take I
Death thought for a minute
Then took the deal
He killed me then and there
But I knew that she would heal
Within a month she was better
The doctors were amazed
From such a quick recovery
When her health was suddenly raised
I watch from in the heavens
As Lucy lives her life
She was the woman that I wished
One day would be my wife
I'm glad I did what I did
For now I live in peace
But my love for Lucy Johnson
Will never ever cease

Judge Me For Me
by Ophelia Scott

I look around but all
I hear is people judging
me saying my clothes
don't match, my hair
looks bad. I wonder
everyday why do they have to
judge me? What did I
ever do? I try to
ignore them but I
never can. All I want
to do is cry. I want
to let all my tears
shed straight to the ground
and then let everybody
still judge me. I have
friends and family that
like me for me and would
not like me to change
and I just have to be me
or no one else at all.

Art
by Bethany Fuller

The beauty is in the eye of the beholder.
The paintbrush is poised
And yet so much noise
The silence is deafening
Put the ear buds in
Choose a play list
Press the play button
And, like magic, the emotions flow out onto the canvass
Such a multitude of colors
All shapes and sizes
Music notes
Faces
Flowers
And random objects that will soon be handed off to my friends
and labeled with ridiculous names.
My life is incredible and I will cherish it forever.

Grandpa
by Joseph Rosson

In the year of 1993
My Grandpa took a flight
Up then down he goes
And it was a very bad sight.
Phillip Arthur Heimbecker
Died that afternoon
His great big huge funeral
Brought lots and lots of gloom.
A great cop Arthur was
A great cop everyone knows
Goodbye great and honorable friend
You will be the greatest everyone knows.

Destroyed Nature
by Michael Avalos

What will we do with nature
It's really getting destroyed
If we don't help it soon enough
"A job well done," will say the android
Nature's trees are getting knocked down
The water's turning brown
Nature has one big giant frown
It will soon look like a messed up clown
Mother nature waters our plants
She keeps us from droughts
When she makes it rain for us
It would make us dance
Her forests are turning into neighborhoods
How will we grow food
She's calling for help can't you hear
Since she's nearly gone, she's filled with fear
Everyday I try to help
It's actually kind of working
When the plant grows
I scream a yelp

I Am a Little Girl
by Emily Cardenas

I am a little girl who lives in foster care.
I am a little girl and my brother does too.
I am a little girl who dances all the time.
I am a little girl who cleans my room.
I am a little girl who sweeps trash under my rug.
I am a little girl who can keep a secret.
I am a little girl who tell everything.
I am a little girl who loves my mother and father.
I am a little girl who loves my foster parents too.
I am a little girl who prays to go home one day.
I am a little girl who needs your prayer.
I am a little girl.

The Day I've Seen You!
by Ashley Hanrahan

The day I've seen you
It's been so long,
I only think about you in a song,
It's time I move on.
Fly away, fly away,
My little love song!

Best Friend
by Payal Thakkar

Best Friends are here for you,
through thick and thin,
Through tough times,
When you can't win,
You share laughs,
You share fun,
You share good times,
In the long run,
Even when you fight,
Your friendship will still be bright!

The Way of Life
by Emily Sours

Today I will give
Tomorrow I will live
Today I forgive
Tomorrow I will forget
Today I will grow
Tomorrow I will learn
You learn many things each day, so cherish them in a new way
You never know when your last day will be, so be brave, be strong, be me

Spring Is Coming Soon
by Abbey Waters

I am a thin, green blade of grass that has just been cut
I am a daisy that is as white as the first snowfall
I am a purple, tiny mitten that has been dropped in a wet puddle
I am a kazoo that is being blown at my 12th birthday party. Ohohhh!
I am the bright yellow sun in the afternoon
I am the baby blue bird that is just about to leave its nest
I am the wind that blows the leaves away
I am a brown grizzly bear that is waiting to attack the fish
I am the snow that kids fall into to make snow angels

Friends
by Ethan Schlapkohl

A friend is someone who is a person to look up to.
If you look up to someone then you have to make sure
that the person you're looking up to is a good person.
If your friend talks behind your back then he's not really a friend he's a bully.
Now my friend has always been with me since we were two years old
and he has never talked bad about me behind my back.
So I thank him for that.
Now friends will always be with you no matter what
if they die in a car accident then they will always be with you in your heart.
So I hope you liked my poem.
Goodbye.

Dirt World
by Emma Wigdahl

With one little ant hill,
It gains more dirt,
From the nasty little ants.
With one little school,
It gains more gossip,
From the regretful little children.
All little ants can build it up and make it worse,
But one, one little ant can stop it all.
It will be a lot of work for this one little ant,
But he won't be considered nasty anymore.
It will be a hard change for a regretful little child,
But she won't be regretful anymore.
As we wander through our lives,
We must step up with pride.

My 10th Birthday
by Sandra Flores

Waking up joyful on October 13 to the voice of my mom
Who needed help on the cooking
My 10th birthday
I ran to the door like a cheetah
To see cars parking one by one on the driveway or yard
They all said hello and gave me a hug, handing me my present
I ran outside and saw my cousins bouncing on the trampoline like little bunnies
My mother called moments later – piñata!
We went by size but I got to hit first because I was the birthday girl
Bam Bam Bam it exploded into a shower of candies
All the kids raced to grab as many candies as they could grab
Then came the cake with a border of fruit and my name
I was about to take a bite when I was pushed from behind
My face covered in frosting my glasses the same
I wiped them clean and went outside to a parade of laughter
And said goodbye to everyone
As they left our house
I went to bed hoping
Tomorrow would be the same

Ode To Bubblegum
by Joe Germany III

Oh bubblegum, Oh bubblegum,
You taste so sweet!
You are a yummy treat
You smell so fruity
Like rooty tooty
I love the way you bubble
Large, medium or
small like a rubble
Oh bubblegum, Oh bubblegum
You bring such joy
You make me a happy boy!!

The Heavenly Dream
by Taylor Todd

As I sit under this shady oak tree I smell the roses bloom.
When the wind blows the pansy petals dance, as if in a happy mood.
The sky a bright pink, the clouds a dark orange.
Across from me is a river which the sunset gleams upon,
making this place even more beautiful.
It just doesn't seem real, this place is likes heaven.
An unseen picture only most people could imagine.
But it all starts to fade and I awake to find it all a dream.

How Summer Came
by Jessica Olejar

I love the rain, how it sounds ever so sweet.
Drizzle, Drizzle, Drizzle.
When its gone, I hear the birds chirp.
I see the rainbows burst.
And I smell Summer.
But I will never forget how Summer came.
Drizzle, Drizzle, Drizzle.

Step By Step
by Kayla Dongieux

First a sock,
then a shoe,
warm-ups now,
just be you.
Practicing at class,
and on the dance floor,
step by step you learn it for sure.
now it's time to show them what you got,
next thing you know your stomach's in a knot,
but just be calm ...
then you'll dance,
Last thing you know,
you prance, with a trophy in your hands!

Sorrow
by Alyssa Bentley

Happiness used to be a part of me,
but now though my tears I can hardly see.
You've left me so now I feel cold and blue,
and I'm really missing you.
I thought your friendship was forever,
and we'd always be together.
But it seems that I was wrong,
now I must stand on my own and be strong.
I loved you very much,
'cause you had a special touch.
You'll remain in my heart,
but at times like this I have to make a new start.
Our friendship and what you mean to me will never die,
I don't want to let you go and say goodbye.
As tears roll down and stain my face,
your friendship and love will never be replaced.
I want to find a place to hide,
life now feels so incomplete without you by my side.
Up in heaven you'll find the way,
a warm place in my heart you'll forever stay.
Now as we go our separate ways,
I know I can live without you for another day.

My Cabin
by Ashley Dohmen

My cabin is very cool
But we don't have a pool
In the morning the lake is crystal blue
The green grass is full of dew.
It has lots of trees
And not many bees
We see lots of deer
But we don't need to fear

Stars
by May Blithe

Stars
Bed of bright lights
Sparkling like a diamond ring
So peaceful

The Old Shoe
by Shane Grice

There once was a very old shoe.
It grew mold and mildew.
The shoe never had grew.
The shoe never had moved.
That's the story of the old shoe.

Life's Flight
by Rachel Fahey

Mine eyes have seen the feather of
The eagle wings that soar above
And as we fly and fly away,
We do not know if passed a day
As we finish this wondrous flight,
We watch as day sinks down to night

Dream
by Olivia Chan

A dream is what you imagine.
The freedom that you have in the dream is what makes yourself who you are.
When I dream, I dream about a little girl finding her way.
Finding what she can do, who she is.
When you find yourself, you find who you really are
and what you have been waiting for your whole life.
Sometimes it is hard to find who you truly are,
but not if you take it one step at a time.

You Liar
by Carla Santiago

You lied to me
Can't you use?
You smashed my heart
like mashed potatoes in a pile,
Not caring for me all the while.
You said about me being the girl
of your life
that was a lie
You smashed me like pie
You broke my heart.
On my heart you left a mark,
You liar! I realized over you, I was higher
You used me.
You smashed my heart
Like mashed potatoes in a pile,
Not caring for me all the while.
If you want me back heck NO.
Just go!
Pack your bags and forget about me
You should have opened my heart with a key,
A true lesson I learned,
my love you burned,
Just go!
You smashed my heart to pieces,
You are even hated by my nieces.
You liar,
My heart for you was on fire,
Not now! You will be the crier.

Quarrel With My Sister
by Sarah Seward

My sister and I had a quarrel,
She refused to hand me my drink.
When I asked her politely she said,
"No, what do you think!"
I repeatedly bugged her,
But she would not budge.
She began to scream and shout,
Though I knew she wouldn't hold a grudge.
She started to call me lazy,
I began to fake cry.
She chased me around with a pillow,
I screamed, "Oh, why do I even try!"
I finally said, "Stop! I'll get it myself."

Spaghetti and Meatballs
by Ali Haynes

My life is like a tangled bowl of spaghetti
Once in a while you hit a meatball
You never know if it is good or bad
Sometimes they are soft and easy
others they are tough and hard
The noodles are tangled
Kind of like the thoughts in my head
Once you untangle them,
They find a way to get tangled again
You get sauce in every bite
It can make it better or worse
I guess you can never change,
The way spaghetti is
But maybe you can cut it up
So it's easier to get through.

Ultimate Running Back
by Jeremy Smith

I am the ultimate running back
I wonder if I will always win
I feel my heart beating on fourth down
I see our team sweating but pushing on
I hear the fans cheering and yelling on the bleachers
I am the ultimate running back
I worry that we won't make the touchdown
I touch the sweat on my brow
I see the faces of my worn down teammates
I pretend I will be the champion of the game
I am the ultimate running back
I understand we can't win everything
I cry our team dreams are crushed
I dream that I'll make it into the NFL
I try to get our team back together
I hope we will win
I am the ultimate running back

The Noise
by Mariah Jones

There is a noise,
a noise that I have heard.
A noise that is familiar.
The hooves beat in a pattern,
like a heart beating against your chest.
It sounds like heaven.
My soul feels as wild and exciting,
as the hooves coming at me.
They stop. They see me.
It's like they are all tamed,
but they're not.
They wonder what I am doing,
but they don't move.
They are just scared of me,
they don't know what I am.
Everyone of them is unique in their own way.
Each one is kindhearted in its own way.
There are some young.
There are some old.
They're horses.

I Am
by Glen Alexander

I am skilled and fast
I wonder if I will make a goal
I hear the crowd cheering
I see my teammates
I want to win
I am skilled and fast
I pretend I am the best
I feel the sweat on my face
I touch the ball with my foot
I worry I will not win
I cry when I get really hurt
I am skilled and fast
I understand I won't always win
I say I did great
I dream that no one can beat me
I try my best
I hope to have a good team every year
I am skilled and fast

Salute To Veterans
by Bryce Johnson

I look around me and I see,
this great land given to me,
by the men who settled the score,
yes, those men who won the war.
And that is why I'm here today,
to make sure they are remembered,
and those that lay under the ground,
never ever to make a sound,
they made the greatest sacrifice,
and when I look around and see,
our very beautiful country,
I think about the men who died,
and made the greatest sacrifice.

The Rain
by Kaitlynn VanGuilder

Afternoon.
Flowers roll with the afternoon breeze.
The grass rolls under the children's feet.
The animals play in the fields.
Clouds roll in.
The sky turns devil-black.
Lightning rolls and thunder cracks.
The children hurry to their homes.
Drip!
The raindrops fall to the ground.
Animals scurry to find shelter.
The world is filled with darkness.
It's gone!
Children come out to play again.
Deer frolic in the wet, grassy fields,
and birds fly to find worms basking in the sun.

That Night
by Alexis Eberly

I still remember that night
that horrible night
when everything I ever had
left me
the house I grew up in
my very own family
and it was all my fault
I take all the blame
I lit that single match
and I threw it away
then I ran, and I still don't know why
I'll never forgive myself
EVER.

Lost To Find
by Kaylee Payne

A legacy with value of gold
A song not sung
A tale untold
Phoenix cries bring light of dawn
With the rising star
A day born, a day lost
The Riddle of the Sphinx 'tis told
An answer sought
But none found to behold
The Poet's tablet, bare as nights
With no story to record
Yet dotted with stars, hopeful lights
Be it beast or myth or song thought gone
All that is lost we must seek to find
Make the legend last, carve it in stone
And slowly we turn to face the light
Now knowing there is more to life
Than fearing what we are sure to find

Bound To the Heavens
by Taylor Liebsch

Walk among us they want
Yet they are bound to the Heavens
Whisper in our ears one last time
Yet they are bound to the heavens
To kiss their child's sticky face
To be swamped up into a warm embrace
To fall and scrape just to feel the pain
To stand on the streets and dance in the rain
To burn their meal they cooked for the night
To run a mile and give all their might
To sweat and greave under a blazing sun
To embarrass themselves just for fun
To write a poem just for today
About how they wished to walk through May
And June and July
Living life with no lie
To leave their heavenly bounds
Get back to earth where they can be found
But they are bound to the Heavens

The First Coming of Spring
by Emily Kriske

As the snow is melting away,
And the green fresh grass
starts to poke through.
The bears awake from their snowy dens,
And yawn with their big, long growls.
Birds fly back for the start of something new.
From Winter to Spring,
The transformation is fascinating.
The animals are reborn,
The wilderness reawakens.
Spring is finally here.

Summer's Day
by Steven Hudgins

Once upon a summer's day
even though we're in May.
Bottom of the 9th, 2 men down
one more strike and they start to frown.
Real big hitters and real little critters
sometimes distract me each game.
I shake it off take a tiny walk
and inhale the nice summer's breeze.
Having some fun making a run
and scoring one for my team.
Once upon a summer's day ...
One strike you're good
two strikes you're fine
Three strikes you're out and you start to whine.
Second batter up first strike down
next pitch, HIT and we're jumping like a clown.
We didn't win, but we didn't lose.
We had a good day's worth of fun.
A good summer's day worth of fun.
Once upon a summer's day ...

Tree Swing
by Rebecca Boehlke

The tree swing sways in the breeze.
Warm summer light filters through the trees.
The swing sways soothingly in the wind.
The children play around on the soft grass.
The sweet smell of flowers permeates the air.
The birds sing beautiful harmonies together.
The sun sets in the Western sky
Creating magnificent colors.

My Wish
by Kelly Cassidy

I wish I were
A river flowing for people
To drink.
Letting the animals play,
Letting people sit peacefully,
And think.

Death
by Anastasia Golter

My name is death and I play this game,
This game of life be ready,
Life is my game and death is my name,
I take you fast, or slow and steady.
I am blacker than night
My eyes with a piercing stare,
In me there is no light,
Call me a black hole for all I care.
No need to infuriate me
For I am already mad,
I shriek like a banshee,
I'd even wear stripes with plaid
You may wonder: "When is my last breath?"
You cannot be sure ... It's up to death.

Golden Buttercup
by Madelyn Johnson

Goldie is spunky and sweet.
I wonder what she feels when we ride.
She hears me urging her to canter.
She sees the woods as we zip through the trail.
She wants to go fast and pass other horses.
Goldie is spunky and sweet.
She pretends she is a person.
She feels happy when we are riding on the trail.
I touch her and tell her she is a good girl.
I worry Goldie will not always be there.
I cry because she soon has to leave us.
Goldie is spunky and sweet.
Goldie understands that I love her and want what is best for her.
I say to Goldie you will always be in my heart and I will never forget you.
I dream about Goldie and I on the trails again.
Goldie always tried her best to do what I said.
I hope she knows that I love her and riding with her on the trails.
Goldie is spunky and sweet.

Superman For a Father
by Luke Rider

When I was little I wished I had Superman for a father.
I would think how cool it would be to fly on his back to school.
Fighting crime side-by-side, the perfect team.
But as I grew older I lost these childhood dreams.
Then one night, I was reading a Superman Comic.
And I visited this wish again.
The next day I was working on a report for school.
For my project, I was to choose my hero and write about them. I chose my Father.
As part of my project I was to write 5 character traits my hero has.
My 5 things were; strength, courage, speed, invincibility, and kindness.
I finished my project and I presented it to my class.
And when I got to the 5 things about my hero, I read them slowly, thinking ...
and in those few seconds, I realized that my childhood wish was never a wish.
But a true statement that could never have been taken away.
I had never realized this till now.
It still amazes me that something so simple made me realize, that I truly do have,
"Superman For a Father."

Untitled
by Logan Tomasek

In February
The groundhog will come to say
The heck with winter

Hannah
by Julianne Carlson

Hannah
Pretty, friend
Helping, talking, laughing
Volleyball, basketball, track, boxing
Walks, jogs, runs
Funny, smiley
Miss Good

I Am
by Tyler Riley

I am fun and love baseball.
I wonder if I will hit a home run.
I hear people cheering from the stands.
I see the ball coming toward the plate.
I want to give it my all and hit the ball.
I am fun and love baseball.
I pretend that I am playing in the major league.
I feel the weight on my shoulders to succeed.
I touch the dirt, squeeze the bat, and swing with all my strength.
I worry about letting my teammates down at great length.
I cry when I get hit by the ball at fast speed.
I am fun and love baseball.
I understand it is just a game.
I say we should do our best and have fun.
I dream of our team winning.
I try to be a good sport no matter if we win or lose.
I hope I play good and all my friends do the same.
I am fun and love baseball.

Black and White Keys
by Kathryn Bray

I am dedicated and determined.
I wonder if I'll ever be a famous composer.
I hear my fingers hitting the keys.
I see the notes in front of me.
I want to be better than the best.
I am dedicated and determined.
I pretend I'm on Broadway playing for thousands of people.
I feel accomplished when I'm finished.
I touch the keys that have brought me this far.
I worry that I will mess up.
I cry when the music moves me.
I am dedicated and determined.
I understand different pieces can be challenging.
I say the hard work is worth it.
I dream about being the best.
I try to practice every day.
I hope everyone that hears my music will enjoy it.
I am dedicated and determined.

Love
by Rynesha Goode

When I say love
I also say romance
When I think love
I say kiss me
When I think love
I say be mine
When I see love
I say that could have been me ...

Wacky World
by Anthony Marquez

As the sun goes by and people fly
there's almost nothing to do, but when
all the dudes are in such a bad mood
then all the food is like goo, this world is so
weird, because of its beard and all of its people are smeared,
this is a wacky world and all of its cities are swirled

Sparkling Starry Night Sky
by Emily Griggs

Twinkling, sparkling, shadowy
In the sky all night long shining
Bright, bold, refreshing stars.

Ice
by Neil Compuesto

Is very cold
Cools down anything it touches
Extremely wet

Life and Death
by Caitlin Pickett

Lonely, frightened,
Family has disappeared,
Miserable,
Irritated.
Hurt, Resentful,
Caught in Men's netting like seaweed,
Disheartened, Harassed.
Yanked from home,
hitting wood platforms,
aggravated, depressed.
Sharp pain in my belly,
unable to bear it,
distraught, bitter.
reviving cool liquid,
trying to swim,
unable to move,
sliding on soft,slimy sand.
My kin,
called by my blood,
sing death to me.
slowly dying,
floating away,
paradise,
hopefully.

Her Glance of Society
by Diamone Hines

Her eyes red with dread every time she thinks of when,
Her soul was black when she takes a glance back,
Of her mind being brown decaying down from hatred,
disgust of violence, from you, me, him, and her
Until this velvet world changes,
We'll be nothing but a checkerboard with all Kings and Queens,
Never wanting to make a move being scared stuck in a little red and black square

Easter
by Mike Bligiotis

Chocolate bunnies, jellybeans, baskets filled with grass,
Hurry up everybody let's all head to Mass.
It's 82 and sunny,
The heat melted my chocolate bunny,
And let me tell you that sure wasn't funny.
We all have met,
The table is set,
I am sure this will be the greatest Easter yet.
The Easter bunny is hopping away,
With many joys of this Easter Day.

Shrouds of Memory
by Bryan Hannah

I walked along the moss covered path.
I could see the intricate design made by the maternal hedges.
I could feel a chill run down my back.
Voices inside of me were telling me to run.
It felt as if my soul left my body.
As I stood there,
I couldn't help but think my soul was already attached to someone else.
My body was motionless, as I felt myself start to evaporate.
As time passed, I was nothing more than a piece of dust.
Wiped from the face of reality.
I ... was ... nothing.
... nothing.

I Am
by MichaelDion Davis-Ruskovitz

I am awesome and gnarly
I wonder if I'll be a pro skateboarder in 5 years
I hear the sound of new skateboard wheels
I see a foot quarter pipe
I want to be a Guinness world record holder
I am awesome and gnarly
I pretend I am in the X-Games
I feel happy when I land a trick
I touch the board that makes me better
I worry I won't be the best
I cry when I fall hard
I am awesome and gnarly
I understand there are things I can improve
I say it's the rider not the board
I dream jumping the X-Games ramp
I try to make everything I do the best
I hope to be a pro skateboarder
I am awesome and gnarly

Friends For Life
by Tamia Ward

The most best friends,
Will last forever,
They stay strong,
To be together ...
From lows to highs,
From highs to lows,
Friends will be friends,
Until the roller coaster slows ...
Friends keep on runnin',
Don't ever go stoppin',
Only infinity miles to go. Until we can't run no more ...

From Sane To Insane
by Travis Wiggins

I'm going from sane to insane. I'm ill in the membrane.
I need a pill to stop my haze. I want my heart to fill with love.
Everyone has gone above I wish I had love.
Should I go home or should I roam my mind it's stuck in foam.
I feel stuck like a garden gnome.
It's starting to rain.
I'm going from sane to insane.

A Death Unknown
by Amirah Raheem

Every day could be our last,
So I hold each new one with a tighter clasp
Because I know with each new breath,
Tomorrow awaits a could-be death
Some never have a chance to say goodbye
We take our last breath, and then we die
But some are lucky, those very few
Who use their time to say goodbye to you
There may not be enough hours in a day
To express the words that I often don't say
Those three little words we hold so dear
Say them now, for, later I might not be here
So every night I sit and pray,
That God will give me another day
And I will spend that day with you
And pray that you'll be here tomorrow, too.

Racism
by Carter Green

Racism is a sin
It can hurt others deep with in
It's like a tiger with its prey
That can mess up their day
So be kind
And you can climb
The different levels
With different kinds

Snowball Fight
by Ryan Klein

Today there is a snowball fight
Joe versus Moe versus Mike.
Ice cold spheres at their side,
They toss a swarm of speeding snowballs.
Loud shouts sound throughout the town
As the trio are pelted from behind a white mound.
Whoosh! Splat! "Ouch!"
The snowballs are like cannonballs,
Flying through the air.
They throw them with such intensity,
That people start to stare.
Snowballs are being thrown so fast,
They're leaping out of the snow.
Finally the battle is over.
But today, there are no winners.
Just three kids,
With lots of frozen fingers.

My Passion For Christ
by Gabrielle Gales

I have a passion for Christ
My passion burns my soul
Like the way lighter fluid burns on charcoal
So Hot!
My passion is for real not fake
My passion leaves me I follow
I live for today because I might
Not live to see tomorrow
Christ has passion , he died for me
Let me rephrase that!
He died for you and me
Took that old rugged cross
While getting beat down on his way to Calvary
Check this out!
You're lying, you're cheating ,destroying your life
Yet still he paid the ultimate price
He sacrificed his life
Now tell me do you have a passion for Christ?

Love Is Not the Only Answer
by Blayney Klein

Hearts are filled with love and care, it's to bad not everyone shares.
People die, and people live, it's too bad not everyone gives.
People teach and people learn, but people still yearn.
Love is not the only answer, even love won't cure cancer.
We have to care, teach, and give so everyone can live!

The Big Fat Frog
by Emilia Weathers

The big fat frog sat on the log in the pond all the day.
All of the day but the log never gave away.

Dreams
by Amir Horton

Aaaah!! Boom! It's like being sucked into a black hole
All you can see is darkness waiting for you
When you fall into this mysterious land there is no way of coming back
Unless you dream
Dream of people, places, and things
And maybe someday you will escape darkness

Basketball
by Miranda Cole

I like to jump
High in the air,
And pull down a rebound
From nowhere.
I like to glide
And steal the ball
Go down the court
And work inside.
I like to pass
Really fast
And score some points on offense.
No fouls
I think
Play defense
With some sense.

Unnoticed
by Julie Macdonald

Unnoticed is how I feel
Confused to what is pretend and what is real
World spinning all around me
I want to show the world what I see
I'm sick of heartbreaks
Sick of hurt
Somewhere in my heart, the damage lurks
Behind the corner and around the cracks
Making me feel like an insomniac
Don't know how to express this feeling
24/7 my mind is reeling
My emotions confuse me
So I go, unnoticed

Writing
by Elizabeth Wordham

For some people,
writing is hard
It's like in a game
when you can't play a card
Then an idea
pops into your head,
and soon you'll be writing
(and may need some more lead)
Words will be coming,
from every direction
You put them together,
they make a connection
Words create sentences
that make something new
Then you'll have lots of writing
That was written by you
If you do your best,
of course you can do it
You'd be surprised what you can do
when you put your mind to it.

Shadow
by Casey Lockwood

A spot of darkness during morning high
And during the night will be forced to die
I always keep pace with you during all the boring things you need to do
I'll always be there when the sun is out
And during the night no need to pout
I'll be back
It's not a knack
I am what people used to fear more than death or mortal strife
I cannot be attacked with a knife
I'm not packaged in a can
Or delivered in a van
I'm not seen in space
I don't have a face
Because I don't need to see
Because you'll guide me

Love It
by Madison Lyndsley

That place I want to be
It may be on a rainbow or in a tree
Love it
It may be in a cloud or on a couch
Love it
It may be in candy land or just in a candy store
Love it
It may be in a mansion or just my house
Love it
Though some people may not have that place to be
In a rainbow or in a tree but the sky is the limit for help
So lend a hand and get them to that place they want to be
That place I want to be is not in a rainbow or a tree anymore
That place I want to be is in a world where there is no crime or war
Like I said
Love It

I Am
by Jesse Adams

I am a strong hunter.
I wonder how long I will live.
I hear people talking.
I sec hunting dogs chasing a deer.
I want a big deer.
I am a strong hunter.
I pretend I'm a pro dirt bike rider.
I feel happy when I'm hunting.
I touch the trees when I walk by.
I worry I won't be good all the time.
I cry only when I'm alone.
I am a strong hunter.
I understand I am very hyper all the time.
I say I got a deer.
I dream about good times.
I try to be a good brother.
I hope summer vacation comes soon.
I am a strong hunter.

Sun
by Indya Page

Gleaming like a bright light
I feel as though I can grab it
Many rays shooting from my palms
I'm almost blinded
Suddenly, dark, ominous clouds covering me
My shine is gone
I fccl dull and lonesome
There is barely a spark of lifc in me
My skin has become pale
How long will this last?
The world is dark without me
This cloud is bringing me to a lifeless light
A big flash!
What was that?
A streak of lightning arcing the sky
This is a thunderstorm blocking my light
The storm is moving away
I'm sparking with life and energy
My shine is back!
My skin gives a golden glow

Love
by Madelynn Williams

Love is when you realize your life is not complete without him.
Love is when you look into his eyes and see the person you want to grow old with.
It is when you feel safe with him,
as though time stops and everything else disappears.
You would go anywhere with him and you would do anything to see his smile.
If he leaves you for five minutes it feels like an eternity,
and when you see him again you realize this is the reason we live, this is love.

Storms
by Austyn Kimbrell

Big flash of lightning
rain pelting at my window
rain, thunder, lightning

Love - An Inspiring Journey
by Jazelyn Shelquist

Love is the final chapter, though it's only beginning.
Mixed with hate, only to find hope.
the hope is harder to find than love.
But ... When the rare love is mixed with the not-so-rare hate,
it brings you hope.
without love there could be no hate,
and without hate, there could be no love,
and without either one, there could be no hope,
so right now, it is only the beginning to a great and glorious future.

Written In the Stars
by Rachel Baum

Imagine what is in the night sky
When the moon, the stars, and planets arise.
Why they are there, are they whispering away?
Do they determine destiny? What do they say?
As the moon and the stars go dancing by,
Do they sing the truth or whisper lies?
While your dreams take over as you lay
The stars align and your fortune waits.

Wonderful Colors of Earth
by Anna Smith

White is the color of clean snow
Red is anger you must show.
Blue is full of sorrow
Purple you can always borrow.
Pink is like a rose
Orange is a pimple on your nose.
Green is the color of grass
Golden is a very good brass.
Yellow is the sun
With teal you will always have fun.

Time
by Kristin Ford

Time is forever ...
It doesn't expire ...
It doesn't get old ...
It stays fresh ...
It remains intact ...
Time can heal or hurts
things ...
Time can heal or hurt
anything.

Fourth of July
by Victoria Haver

Sparks of light,
in the air
Meant to tell of the bravery of men
Who fought to show,
there is no king
So every fourth,
we gather a throng
And celebrate with fire in the sky
The independence won,
on the Fourth of July

My Friend
by Yoko Kofuji

I was blank, empty, a canvas, and then I met my friend. She understood.
Made me laugh, made me cry, made me feel emotions I'd never felt.
Splashing me with her colors.
Purple, sad, quiet, waiting.
Then she's a lazy lounging green.
Later she's lovely laughing joyful yellow.
Red is her rage, which shows only to defend what's important.
Blue are her tears, that she never shows me,
always waiting till I am gone to be blue …
Black is her mischievous part, her blank face, her background.
Orange is her, abstract free, unexpected, unafraid, alive.
White is holy, white is empty, white is boring, my friend isn't this.
No, my friend's a rainbow, a firework in the night sky,
dancing, laughing, whirling, singing, energetic and bright … until she started fading.
Slowly she started fading blending into the night, becoming a star,
becoming a patch in the quilt of the sky, watching me, caring for me, leaving me.
The emotions she showed me flooded.
A river of colors. A huge waterfall. A small stream.
I still have these emotions.

The Fallen Leaf
by Karen Kilmon

The big Oak tree is my very own mother,
I'm the first one to fall of my sisters and brothers.
As I'm falling from the tree like confetti from the sky,
It's hard for me as I'm waving goodbye.
Could this be the start of a brand new beginning,
Or is it just another old inning.
As I was falling from one branch to the other,
I started to miss my mother.
As I kept falling down and down I finally reached the ground,
But when I looked up I saw that I was found.
A little girl reaching out to me,
I couldn't believe I was actually free.
The little girl took me back home,
And while there I began to roam.
She placed me into a book,
Where I began to look.
And to my surprise,
I saw with my eyes.
The mighty Oak Tree,
Looking over me.

The Season
by Anna Thomas

Fallen green tree dead.
Yet life grows in it and out of it.
Fuzzy moist green moss settling around.
In the chilly air, strong tree stares death in the face.
Over the horizon blistering winds and white specks each one holding the Arctic in it.
The moment comes, a chilly blanket settles on the earth.
Life is dying. Dark and empty, colorless earth. Lifeless earth.
This season can take life and give life.

Puppies
by Joseph Hall

Puppies are fun
They like to run
Puppies play
They will chase a ball
And sometimes fall
But always come when you call
Puppies are a pleasure
And mine is a treasure

My Grandma
by Madison Blevins

My Grandma's face is a study in the fall
her eyes and hair are brown.
she visits me at home
and sometimes takes me to school.
She sings me "Twinkle Twinkle" at night
We spend time at church then Outside,
and I play in the leaves while she rakes.
My Grandma Is so cool I like it when she's here!

Untitled
by Judaya Rubertus

A puppy
Furry and loving
Cuddles and barks
Happily
Comet

Cold War
by Grant Lewis

Can
Only
Live
Dictating

War
And
Retreat

Sorrow
by Dakotah Dorholt

Sadness forms part
Of every heart
Revealing itself unexpectedly;
Rendering
Ourselves
Warped.

About Me
by Coralynn Ward

Crazy in my
Own way
Raining from the sky
At home I stay
Later I fly
Yelling to friends "hey"
Nodding to others "hi"
Never know why

Lovely
by Shale Roden

Lotus, a beautiful white and yellow flower
Ocean, majestic sea, swirling wonder, the great mysterious ocean
Violet, wonderful purple flower of the earth, the violet wonder
Earth, the wonderful planet wc inhabit
Lullaby, the sweet sound of sleep washing over you
Youth the magic time in your life where all is possible

Cloud
by Gillian Rucker

A cloud is really fluffy,
It's really big and puffy.
I like to watch it float by,
In the daytime of the sky.
A cloud is my friend,
It backs me up till the end.
A cloud comforts me,
It really inspires me.
There is a cloud up above,
It really helps me love.
There is nothing else around,
That could be anything like a cloud.

The Way To School
by Aaron Warren

In the car,
Down the road,
Across the bridge,
Around the pharmacy,
Among Bascom,
Through the entrance,
Toward right to the drop-off,
Inside the big doors.

3rd Place

Alexis Enacopol

Look Fear In the Face
by Alexis Enacopol

They watch me as I walk upon the stage,
Thinking I'm going to fail,
To fall,
To regret,
As I go on, I show them, I can take what they throw at me,
I am much stronger than they thought I was,
I will not fall under the weight, the pain,
And as I step down, they slowly applaud,
They were not expecting me to achieve what my heart desired,
I looked fear in the face, and won.

2nd Place

Justin Faiella

Cigarettes
by Justin Faiella

Cigarettes are death wrapped in paper.
With all the chemicals inside,
You as might as well pick a fight with the Reaper himself,
A fight you will not win.
Notice how your friends and family mourn you when you smoke?
Because you're slowly
killing yourself
With an eight dollar
pack of cancer.
Why would you start smoking
When you're paying a fortune
for your own slaughter?

1st Place

Jacob Chrestensen

Jacob loves horses,
and has, since watching the movie,
The Man From Snowy River as a child.
They are obviously his favorite subject
when writing creatively,
and he has had the good fortune
of spending time with them up close
as his family has owned several
over the years.

Wild Horses
by Jacob Chrestensen

They are in memories
and we have dreams of them roaming free
Their manes fluttering in the wind
The soft whinny that floats on the prairie that says we are free
But now the whinnies come from barns
and no one answers back

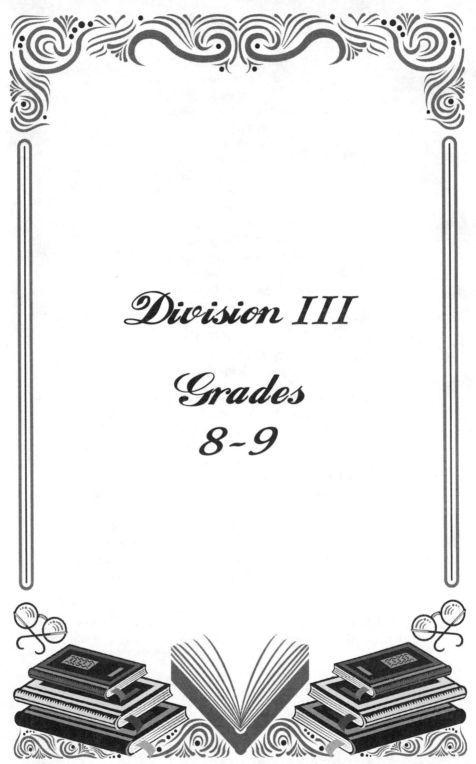

Division III

Grades
8-9

Doubling the Standards
by Lina Gosselin

Be twice as perfect,
in half the time.
Work on it
until it breaks your spine.
Be strong, yet flowy
at the same time.
Stand out of the crowd,
but be sure to stay in line.
Keep your focus,
but also let go.
Do it again and again,
'til your whole body knows ...
Every beet, every word.
So you can shine, while others just glow.
Learn this early to be the best,
Just know good dancers never rest.

Sick of Home
by Cody Fleenor

I refuse to think that this country filled of mediocrity is my home.
I refuse to think that the hypocrisy is just and fair.
I refuse to call this the land of the free and the home of the brave.
When in reality this is the home of cowards and self loathers.
When do we change?
Will Americans ever be truly proud?
Are future generations going to remember us for bravery or cowardice?
I for one refuse to let that happen.
I refuse to say I am a proud American
until the day that I can also say we are the world's dark protector.
A silent watcher that, when it wants, can do great things.
I believe we have the ability to be this, and we were.
Those days are gone.
We don't have the courage anymore
to be the one that everyone looks upon for truth and freedom.
So because of this I'll never be home sick, but I will be sick of home.

The Place Where No Light Shines
by Isaiah Croatt

People hide in the shade of their lies,
hiding the truth from wandering eyes.
Hoping their secret will never be told,
but inside the guilt is growing like mold.
Lying so much can change you a lot,
always hoping you'll never get caught.
People who always hide in the shade,
may have love, friendship, and trust soon fade.
Instead of the shade come into the light,
for if you do this your future is bright.
This is true, so let it be told,
before it turns your heart ice cold.

The Question
by Tyler Sassenberg

"Why are we here?" I hear this question
a lot. It is human nature to
think quietly without giving a suggestion.
Material that makes us ask, Who
made us who we are? What is the meaning of life?
Why does man flourish like a flower
among the weeds while trying to end all strife?
Why does one attempt to build a tower,
though he knows it will crumble with time?
Some don't understand the power of the ideas they believe,
and, like a burglar committing a crime,
they take and give life without them seeing.
But, what is the point of asking this?
After all, life is too short
to worry if your shot was a hit or miss
on the dartboard of life that is such a sport.
Some think of life as a wonderful trip.
Some think of it as a tremendous scuffle or fight.
Yet others think it's a wonderful drink as you take the first sip.
Though we know not the answer to the question, someday we may see the sight.

Life Time
by Ia Yang

Life started with an hour glass
Coming down one by one
Slowly it can go
Making sure everybody has good times
Spending time with family until the last minute
Treasuring the one you love until the end of time
Hoping to give love to everybody that can keep it forever
Wishing for their happiness to last forever
Keeping it until they can't hold it any longer
No matter what, keep spending time together
until the smile is gone till midnight
Till now when the hour glass is done
Everything vanishes
bit by bit
dust is flowing in the air
Nothing in the world
Only picture of memory
Happiness life
Until the end of time

Trouble
by Nicole Blaisdell

White and Brown
Brings me down
Cuddles and kisses
I really miss it
My dog is who
I am referring to
A beagle is he
He sure misses me
When we pull into the yard
I better be on guard
He comes running
And in my arms jumping
He licks my face
At a steady pace
He stays by me the whole time
He thinks I'm so kind
My dog's name is Trouble
I wish he could be a double.

Georgetown Cupcakes
by Giorgina Agostini

My trip to Georgetown Cupcakes was truly not fake,
With so many delicious and scrumptious flavors to take,
Key lime, red velvet, and vanilla with chocolate flakes,
Wanting to choose the right one, I didn't want to make a mistake,
I saw the 2 ladies from TLC that were very kind,
Never meeting a celebrity before I thought I was blind,
My hat, with a sharpie they were willing to sign,
I would certainly remember this day for all time,
Just meeting them my feelings were so bright,
On Facebook, I uploaded the pictures of my day that night,
With so many comments I wanted to hide from the spotlight,
Quickly the day turned to night,
I went to bed and turned off the lights,
Wondering if the next day would be all right,
I slowly drifted away, like on a flight,
I went to bed and all was right.

The Shadows
by Jaryd Tack

The shadows stand tall
They shall never fall
The shadows are here; there's nothing to fear
They shall heed the call!
The shadows shall win the battle of the ages
They cannot be gauged by mortal gauges
The shadows will not yield; they are our incredible shield
They will not be barred by any cages!
The shadows have an incredible story
They charged the enemy for honor and glory
The shadows shone; they amazingly won
They won the battle, long and gory!
Soon their accomplishments grew hazy
The people soon viewed them as lazy
They were burned alive; no one could survive
The people had been driven crazy!
So the shadows fall
None can stand tall
The shadows aren't here; how can't we fear?
No one will heed the call!

Latino
by Alexis Garcia

I am a Latino who likes football.
I wonder if I'll do well in school.
I hear my heart beating.
I see me making the play.
I want to have a cool job.
I am a Latino who likes football.
I pretend I'm smarter than I am.
I feel no pain.
I touch the iron mass of weights.
I worry about nothing.
I cry tears of joy.
I am a Latino who likes football.
I understand that there is no head of congress.
I say let us play.
I dream we won't have a losing season.
I try my best all of the time.
I hope my family will see me play.
I am a Latino who likes football.

In the Wrong
by Kari Ann Peterson

I'm always wrong
Even if I am right, I am wrong
My say in things don't matter
Because no matter what, I am wrong
Always being corrected, practiced or tested
Because I am wrong
It's no use arguing to prove a point
Because again I am wrong
Even when I can prove my answers
I am wrong
People can't accept the fact that they are imperfect
So I am one to make others happy, to feel good about themselves
But I accept it. I'm NOT perfect
But what am I saying?
I'm always wrong

The Best Season
by Jonathan Bentley

When the animals begin to wake from their yearly rest
And when the chirping of birds fills the air once more
And the seagulls begin their flight over the seashore
There comes the season which is the best
And the whole earth is once again blessed.
Immense rains bring the dry ground nurture
And the warmth will renew every creature.
But come summer and then fall to winter, the true test
To see if nature can withstand the freezing.
But it always has, and it always will,
And that is but for one reason:
Come eternity, and there will be always one thing,
Something that no cold can ever kill,
And that is the cycle of the seasons.

Hiding In the Dark
by ShyAnne Skinner

I don't like hiding in the dark
Sometimes it feels like the only choice
It feels like I was locked inside
No chance of escape
Once night falls I feel calm
Through this one small window
I see the light of the moon
Washing over me like a rainstorm
Like a giant hand protecting me
I feel safe when she is in the sky
Then remembering the moon must leave
Darkness envelops me again
I sit on the cold dark floor
Remembering
I don't like hiding in the dark

Searching
by Stefanie Valian

I reached for a rose but cut by a thorn
I wished for a star but fell to the ground
I searched for hope but got lost in the dark
time goes by, days fly past
I'm still lost in the maze not all come out alive
but I'm striving for the breathe of life
longing for the warmth of love to melt the ice away
waiting for the wounds to heal and the sun to shine
I'm looking deep inside to find my voice
and a sign of life below the skin
I'm praying for the strength to get up off my knees
to find hope among the hopeless
to find innocent among the tongues of lie
to fight what threatens my chance at life
even if I look in the mirror
and find the person in the mirror is the only thing holding me down

A Forest In Winter
by Courtney Boone

Twilight falls,
The sky turns as black as stone
Snow gently, delicately drifts like falling rose petals
resting on the stiff arms of the trees,
spreading out ready to catch the first sign of dawn
Warming fire dances into the clouds like a rising spirit eagerly reaching for the sky
Icicles as exquisite as the most ostentatious diamond slowly, patiently form
The darkest point, midnight
sheets upon sheets blanket the town frozen in time
Quiet, as if the world is in a state of permanent silence
Fires still ablaze cast a faint shadow across the town
Sleeping hearts are beating crystals, cold and silent
Morning,
Colors splatter the sky,
Their natural canvas
The darkness slowly ominously creeps away in a foreboding retreat,
waiting to once again overpower the blazing sun
Beaming smiles of the town's children resemble something of a glimmer.
The graze of colors build, the atmosphere a rainbow itself

Hold Back the Truth
by Jordan Hudgins

Racing Heartbeats.
And my rolling eyes quicken.
The sun setting upsets me.
Close the coffin.
The rusty hinges squeak.
You won't miss me.
But missing you makes me cry.
And the tears patter at your feet.
They travel through time.
Somewhere through space.
These words are my only gift.
Don't take them away.
I love you.
And I am sorry.

I'm Too Lost To Be Saved
by Denayha Cotton

I'm too lost to be saved
My aching soul cries for the grave.
Unloved and forgotten, I hang my head in shame.
To me, my life is nothing but a game.
A mistreated child who is always well behaved.
Innocent and harmless, but hated none the less.
A warm smile and a contagious laugh seem real
(but she is just a good actress.)
Brilliant, but invisible, and easy to overlook.
Always at me my parents' heads they shook.
In the sunlight, my eyes reflect my heart of gold.
But since I live in darkness to the world it will never be shown.
Tired and weary my soul carries on in a world filled with hate.
Every night just in case I pray the lord my soul to take.

Undone
by Sommer Sutphin

My heart is bound,
My fate is set,
My doom is sealed.
There's no one left to save me,
There's no one left to try.
As sure as the full moon shall rise tonight,
The Fates have cut the string.

What Are You?
by Erin McDaniel

a purple haze lodge
deep in subconsciousness,
you're a question mark
swaying thoughtfully
without care.
maybe you're something more.
maybe you're something less.
who knows?
whatever you are, you make whoever you meet wonder
aimlessly in what was thought to be a good place.
whatever you are, stop lying and tell people who you are.

Dad
by Tabitha Jackson

When I fell and skinned my knee,
When I had my first chorus concert, When I had a solo,
When I turned ten, When I threw a big party, When you never showed up,
When I broke my arm, When I had to stay in the hospital,
When I needed you most,
Where were you?
When I was in pain,
When I was nervous, When I was alone,
When I succeeded, When I was happy, When I was confused,
When I cried, When I was afraid,
When the only person I wanted was you,
You were gone.
Why weren't you there, when I loved you?

Problems
by Madison Lawyer

Why is everyone fighting?
Is there a way out?
What's with all the people crying?
I may fail without a doubt.
This pain is hard to bear.
Tell me what I should do.
Please someone I'm so scared.
I need to get out of this school.
I have no where to go.
I'm not people's tool.
For all I can say right now is, whoa.
I only came for school.
This problem needs to be able to go.
I can't take it anymore.
This is already the fifth.
Don't pummel me to the floor.

Dawn
by Alex Poirier

The morning air whispers through the many silvery branches of trees.
Breathing the secrets of the world into the needles.
The needles wave slightly, dancing with delight when hearing the news.
Some float downward, their secrets need to be shared with the glass like lake.
The lake ripples when the leaf touches it;
And reverts to its calm state as the information is received.
Dawn is coming.
The first ray of sunshine peeks hesitantly out of the clouds
and dances when it found the all clear.
It stretches across the sky like a toddlers first line;
Shaky and hesitant, but with an beauty that can't be ignored.
The sky then exploded, the different colors of life released into the air.
Golds, silvers, oranges, reds, pinks
Pure as driven snow.
Singing their joy into the light of day.
The lake reflects these colors, pale imitations which still captures the emotion.
Better than any painters imitation.
The light of dawn.

Quitting
by Nou Thao

Wanting to quit so bad but couldn't.
If I do, people will look ugly at me.
They'll make me look bad.
They'll make me feel weak always quitting.
I don't want that to be shown on me.
That's why I act cool.
Act as if quitting never existed.
Keeping it to myself and not letting anyone know.
Only letting me feel all the pain.
Only letting me quit to myself but not to others around me.
Only making it hurt me.
I think to myself, Why am I here?
What should I do?
Should I move on or hold back the pain?
Holding onto my depressed feeling and only quitting inside of me.

September First
by Reed Jones

The date is September first
It's the first day of school
I feel like I'm about to burst
With excitement because it's so cool
I went to bed at nine o'clock
With my friend Ted
Tick tock went the clock as I put on my sock
I knew I had to leave then, I told Fred
Fred is my best friend
He and I made a tree fort
Although we started to bend
The wood so we started to play some sports
Ted is my other friend
He's good with sports
Then we tend
To use up water in quarts
Then when the day is done
We lie in our tents
Counting the fun
We had as the day has been spent

Another Take On a Love Poem
by Amanda Montera

Love lashes at the heart
Twisting and turning
Bleeding and burning
Always leaving permanent scars
Lasting a lifetime, never fading
Knowing this doesn't persuade us
We still dive right into a puddle of burning love
Scorned by the heat, seared by the pain
And yet, we still embrace it.
Love knows no boundaries

Winter Night
by Matt Engelhardt

Snowflakes on the trees
Glisten like stars in the sky
On a quiet night.

Majestic Me
by Ryan Sooknanan

If there was ever a time
I didn't think to see
That thoughts are valued high
This truly amazes me ...
For in my world a bubble lies
Worry and carefree
A castle sits above a hill
And in it you'll find me ...
Proudly sitting on a throne
A robe of fine attire
Crown of gold and jewels I'd wear
Never would I ever fear ...
Servants waiting at my feet
Love and victory I thus meet
A welcome party, food and wine
Divine is this world of mine ...
With a rod, reality reigns
And the bubble disappears
A light rain falls in the distant light
Which brings forth bountiful years ...

Pea Green Walls
by Arre Langer

As I gaze at the pea green walls,
I reflect on the past year of my life.
Me, the perfect daughter, with loving parents.
Then one day they're gone,
A burst of flames swallowed them, and turned their bodies to ash.
I miss their smiles, their warmth,
Now I live in this orphanage;
These pea green walls are the most colorful thing I see.
All the personalities have been turned gray.
I close my eyes and try to remember the sound of laughter,
But all I can hear is crying,
The sad, painful crying of the starving children beside me.
They remind me of my own empty stomach, and I, too, start to cry.
I open my eyes and gaze once more at the pea green walls,
I hear gunfire and loud, wailing cries on the outside of them.
The paint on these pea-green walls is peeling, cracked and ugly,
But it shelters us and keeps us safe from the cruelty of the outside world.
I am an orphan,
And my favorite color is pea green.

Silent Eyes
by Roselyn E. Buensuceso

They think I'm ashamed,
Like I have something to hide.
Their cuts run deep,
As I silently cry.
They call me a liar,
When I am speaking the truth.
They no longer trust me.
If only they knew,
They have been told lies,
And with my very failed tries,
I can only watch my truth die,
Before my very own eyes.

Broken Mirror
by Germaine Lewis

As I walk through the forest of red dust
my eyes begin to water from a familiar scent
the farther I go the sicker my stomach gets
now I hear the scream of what seems like a tortured animal
now I break into a sprint
when I reach a meadow of thorns I see a person running towards me
we both stopped at the same time
when I looked at the person we looked a lot a like
except he looked like he was crying and had just came from a fight
that was when I looked closer i realized it was me

Winter Wonderland
by Eli Castillo

Two horses are pulling people on a sleigh in a winter wonderland.
The two horses are trotting along the snowy, white trail.
The horses have on their blinders so they won't get distracted.
The people are having fun riding in a sleigh through the snow.
The happy driver has a smile on his face.
The people all have smiles on, too.
The ash-colored sky loomed over them.
The blanched snow has covered the ground like a blanket.
The people, driver and horses seem to be having fun
in the ivory, winter wonderland.

Play On
by Brittany Rainwater

Play On
When you're feeling sad,
Think of something funny.
When you're bored,
Do something fun.
When you hit a bump in the road,
Don't give up.
When something that you love ends,
Play On!!!!

Heartbroken
by Brittany McQueen

A broken heart is hard to fix.
Especially when it's in a million pieces.
You might be able to fix half of it.
But there always will be one piece still broken.
Maybe one day that special someone might come and fix it.
But, then again might break it into a million pieces again.
Then you have to start all over,
Trying to fix your broken heart.

Lovely Suicide
by Jannet Hunter

Some say love's a fairytale,
I say love is suicide.
Some say love is eternal and lasts forever,
But I say they are wrong.
Why is it people want love?
I'll never know.
People think it's magical,
I think it's the slowest form of suicide.
It's my lovely suicide.

Fire and Ice
by Maili Steward

Fire burns, ice freezes.
They both cause painful breezes.
Fire is hot, ice is cold
But after a while the pain gets old.
From far away and near by
All I can ever do is cry.
I'm in the embrace of ultimate pain
And all I want it to do is wain.
Past, Present, and Future show
None of us will ever know.
Things frozen or burned will always form
Something new will never be born.

On the Wings of Change
by Jenna Smithson

Caterpillar on the ground,
ambling squirming with no sound.
Innocent to the world of fear,
and the dangers lurking near.
Underneath the melancholy rain.
A bittersweet feeling of sorrowful pain.
Or in the sun that permeates the sky,
when you never have to wonder why.
When hope flies in on a winding breeze,
and drops the worry, along with the leaves.
Then a nostalgic winter drops by.
Color drained from the sky.
Or a caterpillar's metamorphosis
to a butterfly's pure happiness.
Freedom released in the broken cocoon
sometimes things happen too soon.
Change flutters in on the butterfly,
so is it time to say goodbye?

Prairie Upon Green Prairie
by Erik Nystul

Minnesota, bustle
Prairie upon green prairie
The smell of fresh wild flowers
The sound of motors in the downtown
Friendly people are around to converse with
When I rode my bike I slipped and fell down
With the concern of people I got a green cast
Fearing this place won't be the same when I return
My friends steering me in the right directions
Life's now so live it
Clear blue prairie skies
Minnesota, home

American Dream
by Will Bonnell

I've got a credit card with no limit
A bathroom with a TV in it
Just won the game, "Woo!" everyone screams
That's what we call the American Dream
Dad's out working, Mom's still in school
Kids on Facebook learning how to be cool
Cars getting bigger, hearts getting smaller
Every six months the TV gets taller
250 pounds, plus two Big Macs
Smoking cigarettes, by the pack
But with a lot less take, and a lot more giving
We can fix the way we're living
If we all work as a team
We can truly live the American ...
the American dream

Nature
by Olivia Hoppe

Look around do you see the flower
some might see a beautiful work of art
Others see a source of power
Or a symbol of your heart for what magic is bound
Outside do you see the downpour?
Don't make it spoil your day
One would actually go out to play
Or would want to learn to sing in it
What if you see a leaf?
Do you see new beginning?
Some see a source of life never ending
Or a promise the tree is sending
In which will begin its mending
Take a gander at the snowflake
What are you going to do with it
Shovel, sled or watch it fall to the untouched earth
Whatever you chose to do
Nature, will never quit.

The Soldier
by Yoselin Arnez

Empty chairs, empty hearts
Grieving widows, freezing hearths
Six feet under lies your love
But his spirit is above
Gone to glory, gone to fame
Gone to perish, gone to flame
Gone in braver, gone in thrice
Third time gone he paid the price
Giving up all one holds dear
Silent cries, but no one can hear
Lost his children
Lost his wife
Lost his battle
Lost his life

The Simplicity of Life, the Complexity of Longing
by Nasya Davis

To answer the question, how is life? Overall? Well.
Yet there is always need for improvement and always possibilities for pain.
The simplicity that would be, ravaged by humanity's nature ...
Nothing absent save contentment,
Nothing lasting of enjoyment.
No routine except normalcy,
No structure, save the law, unabided.
Lack of peace in silence, who can still the mind?
Many demands to govern bodies, but what shall soothe the spirit?
Ever craving, always filling, but the marrow precedes the heart.
Searching and discovering, discovery lacking intent.
Goodness, afar off.
Perfection, unattainable.
Forgiveness, necessary but unreceived.
Suffering, detestable, yet abounding.
Insanity and crudity, common and acceptable.
Sane of spirit and good of heart: questioned and scorned.
Many changes, nothing new.
Many loves, few are true.
Life lived, unsolved, life to be, unsullied.

Snowflake
by Derrick Goodman

As I fall from the sky
Trees and houses I pass by
As I lie upon the ground I see white all around
The branches on the trees
Dance in the breeze
And as I hear the children
Playing, I get sad,
Because I know for long I won't be staying
As I see the trees
Turn green
I melt away
On a warm spring day

Nighttime Angel
by Brittany Nimety

I look at the moon I look at the stars
I think of the good times and there you are
'Cause you seem like the Angel from God above
To keep me safe with all your love
You're the air that keeps me breathing
A single breath that keeps my heart beating
Without you around my world would crash
You were my wish on that star that passed
'Cause I look at the moon I look at the stars
I think of the good times and there you are
I look at the moon I look at the stars
The times we had have gone so far
You're my angel and that will never change
Your love protects forever and always
But the air is gone and I can't breathe
Please, I'm begging please don't leave
And now you're gone and my world won't spin
I keep on wishing again and again
So come hold me one more time
So the stars won't be the only thing on my mind

My Struggle For Existence
by Holly Youngblood

Year 14, my father was stolen from me
With it, Innocence, Senses, Humanity
Watching him degrade from the strong man, to a stranger hooked to an IV
Time changed hope to fear
Struggle For Existence still idling
I was robbed of knowing that he is okay.
I was filled with regrets.
I was furious because the geniuses in the white coats were incapable of a cure
It was a long period of painful memories, tears, and unfamiliar walls
I will be the girl walking down the aisle fatherless
I will not be given away, instead I'll be watched over.
Year 14, my father was stolen from me
But he was soon turned into my guardian Angel
Struggle for Existence Over.

My Lighthouse
by Chelsea Jones

Behind closed doors I cry,
But no one seems to hear;
Behind closed eyes
I see only pain and tears.
Life has brought me sorrow,
Love, death and war;
It's all just a game
Where everyone cheats the score.
No one seems to care
If they stab you in the back;
'Cause life is like a train
Coming off the track.
No one feels your pain
'Cause no one is around;
All you can look forward to
Is six feet underground.
I thought that was my story,
My final chapter done;
But then I found you,
And it's only just begun.

What Is Fear
by Exzavia Willis

Fear.
Fear is not something to joke about.
It is cruel, harsh and will swallow you whole if not taken seriously.
Fear, is a feeling I have in my gut when I think about frightening things.
Fear is everywhere.
You cannot get rid of it whether it is seen or unseen.
A creature that lurks in the dark or breathes with awake ness in the sunlight.
A simple terror such as vertigo.
Or even a horror that has lived with you since childhood.
Fear may be all those things.
But if fear is not handled correctly it will be your worst nightmare.
Fear will eat you alive and spit you back out with no hesitation.
Fear is the demon inside you that will live forever.
Fear is your life.
Life is to fear.
You may try to get rid of your fear but to do that you must lose a part of yourself.
To live you must have a fear.
Fear is a burden which must be carried on eternally.

Dawn's Picture
by Gabrielle Wolfe

Whispering winds of dawn
sway the brittle branches of ancient trees
this way and that until the browning leaves
make a gentle descent to the green carpet beneath.
A fresh canvas of morning
becomes a backdrop above the scene
tinged with the soft pastels of orange, pink,
and purple.
The single, large, golden globe
rises into the pastel canvas
painting the world
in its enveloping warmth.
A small bird perches
upon a long crooked branch
and calls to the waking Earth,
a call of a new dawn;
rebirth.

Time
by Megan Cunningham

With strong wings
It flies by, It flies by
Along with hope and faith
It claws at happiness
Like a cat at a mouse
Rushes life and
Carries me
As it makes us older
We'll hit rock bottom
But like a feather
We lift back up again
Like the wind
We'll travel for miles
Wrinkles appear
From all the wear and tear
But we still stay young
We stay the kids
Who played in the parks
Our little hearts
That grew to be mature
Stay forever childish
On the inside
Although on the outside
We pretend to be adults
When I wish to stay a kid
It will not listen
It'll spread its powerful wings
And carry me
On rainy days
On sunny days
On cloudy days
And on snowy days
It carries me by
It carries me high
Soaring through
With strong wings
It flies by, It flies by

Winter
by Kevin Wulchin

Snow hugs the cold ground
Painting all things in bright white.
Cold, but fun for all.

I Am
by Jessie Chiasson

I am the future of centuries past
I hear the cry of those I cannot cry for
I see music dancing on air
I want to see the wonders of my world
I am the future of centuries past
I pretend to dance with the butterflies
I feel my whispers carried in the wind's eternal howl
I am sad for the sweet smell of hope that shall not spread.
I cry for my broken heart
I am the future of centuries past
I believe in the power of faith
I speak what I feel
I am the future of centuries past

When We're Old
by Lucy Paige Lotts

we won't be called old,
we'll be considered experienced.
I'll wear my abused chuck taylor's,
and you'll sport a too-big sun hat.
the children will make fun of us,
until we bribe them to keep our foolishness a secret.
we'll go to high school reunions,
that we don't belong at.
I'll brag about true love,
and you'll miss me when you're gone.
our friends will wonder,
at how long we made it.
we'll smile and tell them that,
best friends' love never dies.

Will You Hear Me?
by Cheyanne Neels

Will you hear me if I cry?
Above the thunder of anger
Over the blast of fear and hate,
When help comes not at all
Or when it comes too late,
When streets explode with fire
And hearts grow dead with grief,
When all the sounds are sad
And there's no more relief,
Will you hear me cry?
Will you come before I die?

Anger Is a ...
by Hmongzong Lee

Anger is a very powerful emotion
Anger is an emotion that can attack even the strongest person
Anger is a certain emotion that lives in you.
a power that is hard to control and hard to get rid of
Anger is an emotion that lives within all of us
Anger is an emotion that can be cured by anything that can make the emotion happy
Anger is an emotion that will always stay within us forever
Anger is a very powerful emotion

Unknown
by Alisha Nyberg

The day goes by, class to class
Moving like a shadow, not really there
My mind is gone, thoughts of afar
Almost every minute, thinking of you
Your smile, bright like a star
Twinkling and shining
Your intelligence, far larger than my own
For you know more than I
Your beauty, like that of an angel
Both blinds and makes me see
To think that you're mine, would be wrong
For how could I own something, so close to perfection

What I Am
by Andrea Garcia-Plata

I am beautiful and imperfect.
No one can tell me otherwise.
I wonder what other people think of me,
But I don't bother to care,
what they think of my clothes,
or even of my hair.
What is important to me,
is what I think of myself.
I am beautiful and imperfect,
And no one can tell me otherwise.

Smile
by Natasjha Isidoro

Friends until the end
That's what she promised
And she stayed true to her word
As she was carried away by a faint light
He wiped away tears
For before she left
She slipped her smile into his heart.

The Spirit of the West
by Erin Messenheimer

A moonlit night, the crack of a whip,
A flame like a whisper in the dark;
Thunder on the grassy, rugged tip
Of freedom—the wild and its mark.
An untamable spirit darts through the fog
Like a gunshot at the break of dawn;
A symbol of power and beauty, shod
With fire—a symbol that has come and gone
In man's eyes. We think of how
the West rose and came to be,
Without the shutter of a glimpse now
Of the creatures of hope—wild and free.
Let power run loose for miles—
It belongs in the freedom of the wild.

True Love
by Jessica DeGraw

Look at the sky;
all I see
is your name.
The sky speaks to me;
I hear your voice
when it rains.
When sunlight comes,
your eyes
appear in the clouds.
Your reflection
appears in the
water,
I try to see
me in the water but,
all I see is you.
I no longer can live without you;
you are my one and
only true LOVE

Angel of the Sky
by Steven Tedman

Through cloudy skies,
And bright green clover.
Nature blows its gentle wind.
From up above,
Higher than the clouds.
They rule the land and air,
I see a valiant sense of wonder.
I see an Archangel.
Its beauty and glamour stand out,
The goddess of the sky.
The moon is waning,
The light is fading.
Day becomes a memory.
At nighttime when the land is dark,
Elegance rises to the sky.
I look through the window,
Not expecting to see
An Archangel staring back at me.

My Personal Poem
by Amber Newenhouse

There was this little girl.
Who's mother had left without her children.
The little girl counted on her older sister to take care of her.
Also lived in the house was a man who could make your hair curl.
Late the little girl and her sister and brother were getting beaten.
All they had eaten was bread and water.
The little girl was so hungry she ate dead flies.
At night the little girl and her siblings sat in the corners while sleeping.
Then one day some distant relatives came to play.
They found the little girl crying and covered in feces and bruises.
They realized they had to make a change.
They called the police who came right away.
Foster care was the change to be made.
The three were crying and scared, but they were relieved to be fed.
They received clothes, toys, and a warm secure bed.
The father was out, and a search for the mother was bade.
The mother was found, and years later the family can see.
They are healthy and strong.
Memories may fade, but that does not change.
THAT LITTLE GIRL IS ME!

Spiderman
by Taylor Jenkins

Walking in this room
Full of exhibits of bugs
Feeling the bite from a small creature
Thinking it was nothing
But waking up the next day feeling weird
Saying I'll get well
Then noticing
Long strands of string
Flowing out of my hand
Thinking back to the day
When I got bit
Now being recognized
As Spiderman
Not showing my face when in action
No one knowing the real me
Disguised as
Spiderman

Light
by Anneliese Lee-Reid

When the world shakes
glass breaks
hearts shatter,
light shall come through.
As millions of buildings
lay in ruins
under a cloudy sky,
light shall come through.
Light shall prevail
through and through.
We must all wait,
for it will come soon.
The sun will come
hands shall wave in the air.
When all lights go out
hope will be there.

Poetry To Me
by Cassandra Garvey

Poems that come from the heart
Often you don't know where to start.
Everyone writes them differently
Typed or written, they're all lovely.
Rhymed or not it's music to the ear
You can write them everyday all year.

Prejudice
by Gonzalo Ortega

People hating each other without reason
Racism the worst word I know
Evil the only word able to describe it
Just another day in many people's lives
Ugliness in the world
Discrimination a word that makes my temper boil
In this world why can't we just get along
Carry on with our own lives instead of making others worse
Everything falls apart at the simple utter of this word prejudice

Now It ...
by Sara Lewis

Absolutely Hurts,
Because I Love You,
Caused Me To Be,
Dead Inside,
Everyday,
Falling Tears,
Got Away,
Heavy Hearted,
I Thought We'd Make It Last An Eternity,
Just Another Girl To You.,
Kidding Me The Whole Time,
Love Now I Hate,
Memories Of Us,
No One Else Like You For Me,
Our Love Was Poison,
Perfect To Me,
Quit On Us,
Really Meant Something To Me,
Said Forever and Always But You,
Threw It All Away!!!

Haley Reiter's World
by Haley Reiter

Happy
Almost all of the time,
Laughter is
Essential for the growth of the
Youth of our community.

Ready to learn from the teachers at
Evergreen High School,
Intelligent, nice, and ready to
Teach us and get us ready for today's
Economy,
Ready, set, learn.

Foster
by Jeremy Foster

Foster is awesome!
Oops he did it again!
Sort of smart!
Talented at everything!
Everything about him is terrific!
Right on target!

Military Heroes
by Micaelin Mohler

Missing
In action
Left to die
In a
Thick jungle, thinking
Am I going to survive?
Remembering his family
Yearning for home;

Honoring our country,
Enduring the war; blood
Rushing down his face
Opening a door to a heavenly place;
Ever so
Silent, drifting away ...

His name etched on the WALL today

Vietnam
by Blake Giere

Very loud sickening screams, that's what
I keep hearing.
Even though I'm home from war,
The pain just keeps on feeding. It's
Now been twenty years and I'm
Alive and staying strong, but I owe
My life to the men that saved me from the Viet Cong.

3rd Place

Amanda Eunpu

Submission
by Amanda Eunpu

Her eyes search the form expectantly,
Trying to find the rules and regulations
That tell her what she may write about.
Voila! There it is!
The sky's the limit.
Her hand takes its place poised above the blank paper in front of her,
Waiting for the inspiration that is sure to come.
It hits her like she knew it would,
as hard as a rock and as strong as a hurricane.
Her hand flies across the page,
jotting it down as swiftly as it comes to her
And then her hand stills.
She folds the paper slowly and seals the envelope hesitantly.
Though she may not know everything,
She knows it won't win, but that is not the point.
She knows her heart was in it, and she knows
That is the only thing that matters.

2nd Place

Katie Elks

Ponies and Mustangs
by Katie Elks

Let them be ponies,
All pampered and pretty,
Yet harnessed to their master's will,
I'd rather be a mustang,
Running free, wherever I please,
No one forcing me to follow,
Learning to stand on my own,
Not having things done for me.
Living for what is best for me,
Not just what everyone wants.
To be a mustang, and not a pony,
Would be the right thing for me,
Being free to be my own person,
Not harnessed to be something I'm not.

1st Place

Mahathi Ayyagari

Mahathi is an avid reader
who especially enjoys Greek mythology.
Playing piano and singing are also among her many talents.
She is currently taking a journalism course,
as she intends to work for her school newspaper,
and when she isn't spending time with family and friends,
she studies French, with dreams of one day visiting Paris.

The Forest of Athens
by Mahathi Ayyagari

Just outside the bustling city of Athens,
lies a forest full of surprises.
Flowers dance, branches sway.
Graceful centaur's hoof beats are followed by whizzing arrows.
Satyrs persistently court giggling dryads
while the sleepy scent of the anemone poppies,
stained with the crimson blood of Adonis, envelopes your reeling mind.
You might just hear the nymphs' euphonious laugh drift from the trees
and combine with the melodious tunes of the panpipes
or feel the roaring waterfall's mist kiss your cheek.
Nearby, glistening sirens splash their tails in the cool water, calling to you.
You want to follow so very badly.
Pixies buzz around your ear, laughing at your foolishness,
but stop at the soft-hearted sound of a
babbling brook in time with the lyres of the muses.
You find yourself lost in a magical world, where every turn brings adventure.
Welcome to the forest of Athens.
Enter if you dare.

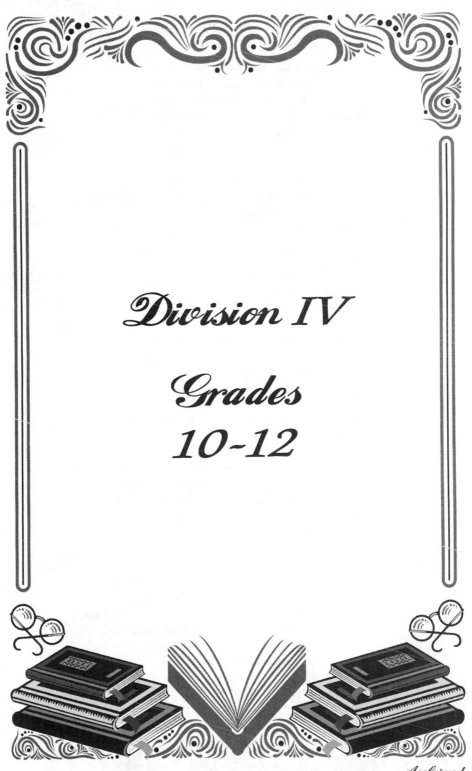

Division IV

Grades
10-12

A Mouse For a Sly Old Cat
by Nana Asihene

A tiny mouse looks over a window
Fantasizing over a family meal
Reaching his sensations out,
He glares at the scraps of meal left before his eyes
His fantasies get larger
Forcing him to go for the food he sees
Luckily for him the family cat was fast asleep
He jumps into the house
But less did he know he was headed right into the cat's meal
Upon his arrival to his regretted destination,
He witnesses the deceit of a sly old cat.

Lost: an Elegy
by Austin McGlothlin

What happened?
I woke up this morning and you were gone …
I had dreams that you had died …
And now I find it's true …
I pray every morning …
Before I walk out of my room …
That you will be there… in that old armchair …
And then I find that I've had no dreams …
And I become lost …
I don't know what to do … or how I'm going to live …
And then I have the dreams that you are there …
That I walk out of my room and you're in that armchair …
You would try to stand up but I wouldn't give you time,
I would kneel down to you hug you for a first time,
Though my excitement made me anxious …
Then my mind makes it clear …
That when I would wake up you would disappear,
And then I am crushed by this cruel dream,
Though I still keep my faith that you are watching over me.
I would kneel down to you hug you for a first time,
Though my excitement made me anxious …
Then my mind makes it clear …
That when I would wake up you would disappear,
And then I am crushed by this cruel dream,
Though I still keep my faith that you are watching over me.

Society's Creation
by Nicole Bragg

I am the monster,
The bloodsucker
Creeping under your bed,
Squeaking your staircase
I am the monster,
Outcast of society
Laughter
Rejection
I am the monster,
Looking for nourishment
Hiding in your closet
Refuge
I am the monster,
Branded by society
Forever isolated…
Dare to be different

Beaming Through My Tears
by Gina Van Thomme

A cloudless sky showers rain
There is no wound, yet so much pain
The sun shines in the dead of night
Life feels like the blackest white
A hurricane in a lake
This is so real, but seems so fake
Like driving on the left-hand side
So counterfeit, yet bona fide
This mystery enfolds us all
Like a spring that's in the fall
It is a Q without an A
Going to work on Labor Day
Kind of like a frozen flame
A million invitations, yet no one came
You 'will can did' every 'would could should'
The best things can never be understood

Irrevocable Susceptibility
by Cheyenne Folk

A passing glance begins my mischief,
I get too close, and then resist it,
My poison lips persuade you in,
Her heartfelt love, it never ends.
Consume me like a crashing wave,
Spit me out, alone I'll stay,
She'll never love you like I do,
My love's a sin and hers is true.

Frozen Memories
by Sarah Kerr Watts

The solid presence of my siblings
On either side of me,
A passage of time,
In one single moment
The warm sea breeze wrapped around me like a blanket,
The soothing sound of the waves and the salty ocean air
Surrounded me in a cocoon of memories filled
With little girls running wild.
The warm sand slipped between my toes
As I gripped the loosened leather of my sandals,
Like a tether to the ghosts of my childhood
Building castles at my feet.
The salty oceans air surrounded me as
The soothing sound of the waves
Whispered long forgotten messages
Of sisters sharing secrets in my ear.
The vast never ending ocean in front of me
And the line of houses behind,
Like a book of old pictures
Long forgotten.
The chatter of my relatives,
With their colorful umbrellas and chairs,
Like the murmur of old stories
Filling my heart.
The solid presence of my siblings
On either side of me,
A passage of time,
In one single moment.

I Am
by Phillip Scruggs

He is the result of a mighty people's oppression and prolonged injustice,
He is the hope and future of his ancestors who built a nation from tears and bondage,
The cries and groans of the past are engraved within his heart,
And with him he carries a burden cursed upon him centuries ago,
I am him and he is I,
He inhabits a world where many want to see him fail and cease to grow,
He inhabits a world where the clues of the past cleverly disguise themselves,
Almost as if they weren't there at all, but they are just as prevalent as long ago,
However, his soul is stalwart such as his ancestors
and just as they did before, he will prevail,
I am him and he is I,
He hints a stench of cruelty and bitter hatred targeted at his soul,
However just as his ancestors, he shines a light far brighter than that of the sun,
And overpowers the darkness and horrendous images that try to surround him,
For, with his faith and love of everything that is free, just like his ancestors,
he will reach the promise land and continue to grow,
I am him and he is I.

Ten People Looking At You
by Breeana Johnson

What happens to you when you are in a room, with 10 people looking at you?
What happens to you when you are in a room, with 10 people listening to you?
What happens to you when you are in a room with 10 people...
who can't understand you?
Well, for a stutterer like me, a lot of things go through my mind.
For a stutterer like me, it's challenging saying even a sentence to my peers.
What I have to say becomes consumed in what I want to get out.
What I want to say gets blocked before it comes out.
I worry about what others think; my heart races, and I think quietly to myself,
"Why me?"
But self-doubt does not stop me having to speak to 10 people in a room.
My lips get dry; I need some water. It's already been 10 seconds; I need to start!
I open my mouth and hope for a phrase, something to ease out!
I need more time! I look at the clock, oh no! It's already a quarter past nine.
Already I've said nothing, and 15 seconds have now gone by.
I close my eyes, deep breathe, and begin.

27-153
by Thomas Stevens

I have no name.
No name's deserved by me.
I am simply to be known
As number 27-153.
And this is my story,
As you shall see,
About the twelve hundred souls
Who passed through 27-153
Six million Jews,
Five million others.
Some, someone's brother,
The rest are their mothers.
The swastika,
The Third Reich,
Exterminating those
Who are not alike.
Trying to put barbed wire around the world.
Imposing such suffering on the once free.
I am such an individual,
I am number 27-153.
I used to work with cattle,
Loading them on the train,
But not anymore.
On the yard, is such pain.
Why must I be forced to inflict such pain,
All my brothers and me?
As they all must clamber and suffocate
Aboard I, 27-153.
Most smother and die,
Amidst the flesh, my wood, and steel.
Those who didn't wish they had,
For what's ahead, men aren't meant to feel.
I can feel their agony,
Through the floorboards,
The wood, and the rivets.
I'm sorry, victims of the SS hordes.
I'm not supposed to feel,
But lately I find,
As the Deaths-Head express,
Their pain becomes mine.
I'm sorry for the suffering I cause.
Even I am not free,
The transporter,
And the passengers of 27-153.

The Girl I Can't Forget
by Cody Vlaminck

I wake and realize that I can't get her out of my head,
The way she talked,
Like a guardian angel telling you that she got your back,
The way she walked,
Like the grass in the African savanna where the lions lie
How much she liked to talk about mythical creatures
Vampires, Witches, Werewolves, Succubus, and all that kind of stuff,
I miss all the time she was afraid of losing me because she was gaining weight,
I miss telling her "I'm not one to judge on the size of a girl's body,
I only judge the size of her heart,"
She calls me a sweetheart
and said, "Any girl you will ever have will love you very much,"
I miss listening to music with her in the car and on the computer,
Her voice was amazing it knocked me dead every time she sung a song,
Even if she didn't know it,
Her smile made me feel like it was a dream all around me,
I'm glad to have her in my life,
Cause it was the best six months of my life.

September
by Brittany Dwyer

Like the best-kept secrets
stay in the mind.
Like a heap of brambles,
left intertwined.
Like a busy world spinning
a little too fast.
Like the unfolded scene,
left waiting to last.
Like the creativity
of an artist at work.
Like the mind of a child,
which will silently lurk.
Like a dream once remembered
is beautiful to greet.
Like the taste of watermelon
is delicious and sweet.
Like a one-step dance
with a step added in,
I'm left falling for you
Again and again.

Hands
by Chris Allan

These hands of mine, curious and warm to the touch.
These hands which move and grab, crush and smash.
These hands of which are mine, I know.
Though they are also on their own.
Free to do as they wish. Free to hold, touch, and kiss.
But I can't stop these hands, for they are more than just my own.
They inch their way from wrists to grab hold of the lyre of Orpheus.
To have the wind glide between their legs.
To touch the walls filled with secrets which excite their hearts.
Whether they perspire, aspire, whether or not they conspire
or go as far as to build an empire.
It should be common that these hands of ours be joined.

Lose All Control
by Annika Lind

Perfection
My one true enemy,
With its sparkly smile
Of pride, and
Its gleeful moments of joy,
That's when I lose all control.
Emotions flying – unstoppable –
Like the wind, tearing
My mind apart
From the inside out. Like a disease.
That's when I lose all control.
Understanding of it sliding out
From under my feet.
I feel like I'm falling,
A million miles a second.
That's when I lose all control.
Hiding my true form
Under fakeness and cruelty.
Not finding my voice,
Unable to stand up for myself.
That's when I lose all control.
One day will change this
Moment in time, this second in
Eternity. But for now, I will hide my true self from you.
That's when I will lose my control.

Just Because ...
by Olivia Adams

Just because I'm young
Don't turn your back when I speak, because I'm not unknowledgeable
Don't rub me on my shoulder and try and cover the truth,
because my feelings won't get hurt
Don't have only an ear to hear because I can't be misunderstood
Just because I'm young
Doesn't mean I don't know about life
Doesn't mean I can't teach the young, my peers, or my elders
Doesn't mean I won't at the least try
Just because I'm young
Try and give me a chance
Can't wait till I get older
Just because I'm young–please take me seriously

Where Death Takes You (R*evolution)
by Christina Abbott

In a little hollowed out tree lies a gasping man, holding tight to its branches
air rejects him, shriveling him like a prune, his ribbed wings fight to break free
the balloons of his eyes burst from their holes
glue is the only thing holding them in
a dark echo erupts from the hole beneath
a man riding on a darkened carriage speeds by with his devils behind
the man laughs
and death's true form shows
a man in blue
the toga down to his feet
nearly Victorian by his eyes alone
another laugh erupts
and a volcano burst
from within the tiny city of Mouranders
Balloons escape their bounds and an angel is born
from the ashes of another
freed from mortal bounds
a dark angel is crowned

Scorned Lover
by Caroline Boles

With eyes the color of crimson fire
With lips the solidness of stone and ice
Her hair long and thick color of the moon
With pasty white skin And a smoldering gaze
She sits on the roof
Senses strong as a wolf
She waits with a dagger in her hand
She didn't want to
She cried bloody tears hoping
For another answer
Guess it wasn't meant to be
The door opens
She hears but does not look
Only picturing the light in his eyes to fade out
Wiping her face bear
She flicks her wrist and watches him fall
A hand on her heart and eyes on his blood
She pulls the dagger out of his skull
And she walks away with a heavy burden over her heart

Jet Ski
by Taylor Olson

The purr of the starting engine as I slowly float away,
I know just how to rid myself of a scorching summer's day.
A damp breeze replaces the heat within the calm;
I feel the power surging up from underneath my palm.
And so begins this battle, of power and control
As the speed takes me far away from just a calming stroll.
I fish tail right, I fish tail left, then circle on a dime
The roars from below let me know that it detects my crime.
I feel the force that drags me off but I put up a fight
My whipping hair and beating heart tell me everything is right.
Then suddenly I'm flying into the blue abyss
I feel the rush as I'm greeted by its cool and calming kiss.
I break the surface and take my breath ready to start again
And staring at me waiting is my ever ready friend.

Grace of the Storm
by Patricia Inman

Thunder rumbles in the distance.
Rain pounds the rooftops.
The wind whips and howls like banshees.
All combined in the darkest hours of the night.
Trees ripped by the roots.
Houses gone from their foundations.
Windows broken from their sills.
All missing in the night.
Lightning flashes across the sky.
Drums echo in the deep.
Ice falls from the heavens.
Destruction is imminent.
Beginning anew.
A bright new dawn to clear the sky.
Silence resonates through the land.
Hope and love are born.

In Need of an Angel
by Kayleigh Lawson

In these painful years,
The things people say burden in many ways.
Always finding imperfections, making sure everyone will see.
It hurts to know these things they think of me.
They hardly even talked to me before,
But only offering jeers and laughter to my ears.
They, nor my family know I cry
When I'm alone so none can know my weakness,
And I pray—
Pray that someday I'll be different and likable for them,
That the hurt won't carry over to tomorrow.
And I lay there and realize I'm not the one that needs to change.
I will not be someone else.
I will be me and my prayers change,
That I please just have the strength to move forward.
As these insights hit me, a weight was lifted
Off my shoulders and into helping hands.
An angel here to help me,
Sent by a god who loves me.
Peaceful, I will rest in the arms of my guardian angel.

Fade To Black
by Taylor Kintigh

The whole world is a dead-black.
That feeling of safety is gone,
the world is in so much chaos,
there is nothing I can do about it!
But there is one hope, a special day is now here,
The world is now a blinding white,
With purity and happiness filling every heart, soul and mind.
Where brothers and sisters, friends and enemies
can join each other and put aside all troubles,
see eye to eye,
sign an armistice, for one whole day.
But that feeling is all for naught;
The death and despair begins again, and the all the people,
Fade to black!

Big and Red
by Laren Minton

The sky is getting darker.
The rainbows fade to gray.
As the rain starts to steady, the animals hide away.
One large creature has nowhere left to go.
The rain is getting harder.
The thunder starts to roll.
The strange, red, being tries to run and hide.
Nothing will conceal him because of his
color and size.
He falls in the mud.
His eyes fill with tears.
He yells out for help …
nobody hears.
The 'friends' he once knew now watch from afar.
The lighting strikes fast, and leaves him with scars.
His body goes numb, his eyes become dry.
The thunder, rain, and lightning have left the sky.
The rainbows are back, he's floating on a cloud!
He smiles, happy again, and looks slowly around.
His body is below, big and red on the ground.

Held
by Harley Woodard

I want to be held,
To be shielded from pain,
I need you to protect me
Because ... I can't do it on my own
I hate you but I love you
I want to be held
so, all the bad things
will go away.

Zippidy Doo Dah (Green)
by Michele Borsari

Zippidy Doo Dah has the exuberating taste of a green apple,
a honey crisp to be exact.
Munching sounds like the motion of mastication in the distant land;
joy fills the ears of young ones after they hear each bite.
It has the odor of a hot summer day.
Zippidy Doo Dah is the color that you would see in Emmet's room.
Ah, cucumbers and limes are the images that come to my mind
when I think about Zippidy Doo Dah.
Zippidy Doo Dah has a great Zing!
As well as a great Zong!

Broken
by Kelli Price

In the beginning, these hands were trying to quit shaking.
Then these hands were trying to understand how they fit into yours so perfectly.
Now, these hands are trying to wipe away the tears.
In the beginning, these eyes were trying to grasp your perfection.
Then these eyes were trying to understand how they got lost in yours so easily.
Now, these eyes are trying to hide the tears that won't stop falling.
In the beginning, these lips were trying to make sense when they spoke.
Then these lips were trying to understand
how they melted with yours so wonderfully.
Now, these lips are trying to forget the taste of your kiss.
In the beginning, this heart was trying to believe it could trust again.
Then this heart was trying to understand how it was yours so completely.
Now, this heart is trying to pretend like it's not unbelievably broken.

I Want
by Caroline Bunjer

I want to tell you,
it wasn't your fault.
I didn't mean to blame you,
for all you couldn't be.
Now it just seems easy to only blame me.
I never meant to hurt you,
I know i made you cry.
It couldn't have been easy,
to almost see me die.
I never meant to walk away,
from our family home.
I didn't mean to break your heart,
and leave you all alone.
I never meant to take away,
all you ever had.
All i really want to say is,
I love you dad.

Engulfed
by Samantha Rafalowski

Dive down … Deeper
Submerging into the warm, milk-chocolate pools
Of beauty de-emphasized
With such a label as only "eyes."
Search onward … Further
Drowning peacefully in a vast space
The purport of a benevolent soul opulently adorned
With wisdom, acumen, and erudition.
And still such clemency yet unknown by the preponderance of man
But breathed into this man from the start.
Respite now … Respire
Appreciate what has been seen
Regale in the discovery of such a person
Just a person. But with a heart of resplendent fire
For he has opened the gates guarding his eyes
And vindicated the presence of something genuine
Yes, something pure exists in the world.
Ensconce again … Silence
Float back to the surface of such depth ascertained
Engulfed once more in a soothing quiescence: his soothing quiescence.

The Snow Globe
by Russel Peterson

Plastic Ballerina—
In a crystal glass dome.
A glitter arena—
How she twirls in her home!
On an old, dusty shelf.
The snow globe's lone figure
Waves her doll-like elbows:
Dances, prances, a gesture!
Performing such grand shows.
Yet, she looks so morose!
Trapped in a prison sphere,
Blizzards always blowing.
Kept in a state of fear,
Her pain clearly showing.
Sadness wells up in me.
If only she had luck!
Or could jump to demise:
Become shards when she struck
And oozing liquid lies,
But life is rarely kind.

The Fight
by Maddie Doering

The words I left unsaid
Were racing through my head
Oh why did I have to doubt
The things I wanted to shout?
You make me so furious
The way you are always delirious
To our problems, to our fight
Don't you see that this is not alright?
But you are not here now
And with myself I shall take a vow
Never to skip a word, not a vowel
Even if it hurts I will not throw in the towel
You won't win, you can't win
I'm done with your thick skin

Tears From Your Heart
by Heather Middleton

Tears are words from your heart
That can't be spoken,
Sometimes your tears stay with you
You cry every day thinking of him
That you are so heartbroken without him
You see him, and feel him next to you,
And feel being in his arms right now
He was smiling at you
You were smiling back
He feels so real to you, but
You were just dreaming …

Scar Garden
by Jared Iler

The seconds blend into minutes as they fade into days
The colors don't shine; they're all a dull grey
She fell so deep into depression that she honestly can't remember
What it's like not to live life off of confession
Each new day stole a piece of her mind
Staring patiently at the wall as if there's something she'd find
There's nothing more painful then failing at life
Hung the "No Vacancy" sign and shook hands with strife
And all this has taken its toll
She can't reach for the sun; it's just too cold
It must be a burden to lie to yourself
Convince your mind that you're fine and in optimal health
I know this sickness has you out in the cold
Simply not trusting those offering hope
But go home and rest, 'cause home is where the love is
Life has been nothing but a struggle that you've been trying to depart with
I always looked up to you as a fighter
You're starting to slip, don't let go, hold tighter
But what it takes for her to face a day
I can only hope to be half that brave.

The Stargazer
by Kaitlin O'Brien

The eye crinkled shut foretells
Worlds far apart, and yet so near
And what wonders shall be beheld
In that great brass looking glass
Held so dear.
And the lips slightly parted reveal,
The night is favorable to thy gaze,
Far into realms a lifetime away

Sorry To End Like This
by Ava Hull

We will be free, the wars will end
I will stop our people suffering, that's what she said
An old friend of mine named America
We were once tighter than handcuffs clinched on murder victims
Or so I thought
But somewhere in between our false representation of a true friendship
a cloud of betrayal took over
America you were once my best friend
The strongest girl I had ever known
My biggest supporter when times were tough
My kindest friend when rudeness kept punching me in my face
But something happened during the time
you began to get in all those wars with our foreign allies,
your appearance began to fade, you were becoming annotatable
I began to see your true colors
I believe I really began to see it when you turned on me and on ours
Ha I began to see your true colors and they were not bright
My eyes weaken each day to see where you have gotten us
Your strength faded, your courage weakened, how could you let this be?
You assured all your people that we would be free as white doves
flying into heaven with the two big gates wide open
How could you let this be?
So many of your people were counting on you to make them strong
To help them find the voice they never thought they had
I'm done with you America, you can call this old friend
when you have found that strong loyal soldier I once knew
But until then I'll be making my way in this world being the strong, tough tree I am
Sorry it had to end like this

Feelings In the Dark
by Becky Kromm

Shadows walk in my heart.
A bloody dagger stabbing it at every beat.
You caused this, you created this hell.
I gave you my life, you gave me this paradox.
But life goes on, after all.
You lost the one thing that meant the most to you,
You just don't know it yet.
I have moved on, but the question is, have you?
I see how you look at me, your eyes puzzled and perplexed.
Your actions cost you my love and affection.
How does that make you feel?
One day you'll understand, but by then I will be far gone,
And you, you will be nothing but a faded memory, if that.

Teardrop On a Dress
by Veronica Lilgreen

The most exquisite dress
Made for her who's flawless
It fit just right
All eyes lay on her
In the spotlight
Dancing, the dress
Matched her every movement
The dress knew its accomplishment
It almost seemed apart of her
Its pride increasing as she dances
Her beauty? all were sure
Soon she twirled off the dance floor
But the dress wanted more
She gave a gracious smile and parted
The dress, so vain hearted
Clung to a rose bush
Begging for oohs and awes
Once the girl tripped
The dress it ripped
And a teardrop fell on the dress

The Flower
by Jacob Ogle

My eyes are vividly
Lit, my mouth pressed
Into a pleasant smile, and
My body jitters with excitement
But these are only a cover
For my heart sings of
Pain, loneliness, and death
For I watch a beautiful
Flower die, but I must
Act prim and proper to
Barely keep it alive
Each day I show love
And affection to this flower
I water it and fertilize
It but no matter what I
Do it slowly wilts and
Decays
As I scramble to catch the fallen petals
I hopelessly watch as the
Flower dies and decays to nothing

Shall I Compare Thee To a Winter's Day?
by Lupita Mosko

He had such an inviting face
You'd think his heart was made of gold
He seemed perfect but he was out of place
Inside he was bitter and cold
He had looks of an angel and a soul of ice
Everyone couldn't help but fall for his smile
Unfortunately his charm came with a price
His frozen heart couldn't even love for awhile
He found amusement in tearing people apart
Hurting others like he once was treated
He messed with their mind while playing with their heart
I had fallen for him anyway, my efforts defeated
I was left heartbroken by the brokenhearted boy
Who loved the girl that had played him like her toy.

Little Red Hen
by Benjamin Haugmo

Urgent, wantful desire
for nothing more
than a tree house.
But not to have to build it.
A burning, hated disgust
for everything
about my situation.
What is a fourth grade doing
twelve feet up in the air?
Holding up two by fours
and hammers and pounding
and pullies
and linoleum flooring
and secret trapdoors
and ooo, that
is a nice tree house.

Mary Jane
by Miatta Kingg

Frigid wind blows against my skin.
I kneel down; my frosted fingers gently trace all eight letters of your name.
If only you were here.
I stare at the laced embroidery that loosely coils the bouquet of purple flowers.
As that was your favorite color, mine too.
Your grandson misses you dearly; sometimes I do as well,
Although you and I have never met, until now.
If only you were here.
On his dresser, lies the last captured memory of you and him.
He was about ten and you had already began to sprout gray hair.
I blink my eyes to hold back the tears. How rude of me to cry in front of you.
I came to you for your blessing, as your grandson craves to tie the knot.
No words can begin to express the love we share.
I have only dreamed of the words that you and I would speak.
Oh, how I wish you were here.
I can hear the robins now, singing to us from a nearby branch.
Soft rain trickles on to your tombstone.
I place my own bundle of flowers against the eight letters of your name.
I rise from the ground slowly, walking away, only to glance back.
And I think to myself, oh how I wish you were here.

Nature
by Kara Dafin

The Shield i put up is no more
feelings i get from this freedom give me hope
and joy.
Its like rain being released from the sky.
or sun reaching out of the clouds, grabbing daylight.
Pain that was once as annoying as the constant chirp of a cricket,
has now subsided to the sound of a blade of grass blowing in the wind.
my only tinge of regret comes from you.
and in this peace and serenity
i still have the thorn in my side,
highlighted with your calm, sweet
breath. And the thought of us.
through the haze of pain my true
happiness waits for you.

Where I'm From
by Maggie Walstrom

I'm from a family,
Whose ancestors were involved with gangs and Al Capone,
I'm from a family,
Whose ancestors helped hide Anne Frank,
I'm from a family,
Where my great grandpa did moonshine,
I'm from a family of artists and writers,
I'm from a family of athletes,
I'm from a broken home,
I'm from a family that's raised by an awesome mom,
I'm from a family,
That loves to say "I love you",
I'm from a family,
That likes to listen to Linkin park, Beyonce and The Black Eyed Peas,
I'm from a family that's always busy,
I'm from a family that loves to have fun

Shattered
by Alexandra Leaskas

It hit hard. Sorrow, sight blurred, the heart shattered.
Unexpected in action, felt from the vibe–never thought it'd be followed through.
How? I don't know. Why? Why? Why?
Why does this hurt stay? Why can't it just go away? I ask.
I wonder why I have to go through it, I wonder how to deal, what to do.
I wonder when it will stop,
that wave of butterflies and emotion from my stomach to my eyes.
All sorrow flows out in the form of a tear, but doesn't go away.
No matter the amount I pour out of my eyes,
no matter the words I speak, I can't heal it. Why?
Why is this fire not dying out, but taking blows to be killed, murdered, slaughtered?
It lives so strong and has so much will, but I am beat so low.
Hope is so low, sorrow so high. It won't die, it won't heal.
A wall, a dead end. My heart a shattered standstill.
I try to piece it back together to be one and whole again, but no control exists, I can't.
Impatience around my next corner, anger and desperation for sanity, for control.
What now? Emotions and truth were blinded by You Destiny.
But now, this Destiny is just a friend.

Love Resembles the Woman
by Jacob Leavenworth

The tender swell of the ocean
Caresses her ginger sweet hips
The delicate white virgin motion
Finds peace on her calm spoken lips
Love resembles the woman
A rose with a thorn
A written page torn
A wintry pure heaven touched morn
Solace is found in the moment of time
When emotion takes wing and ascends to its prime
As dreams grasp at the face of illusion
The ephemeral ember burns bright
There's a cold silver moonlight-clad soldier
Dictator of golden-rich fruits of the light
Find me asleep in a flurry
A flurry of amber paint reverie
A storm of a man who is finally free
A mosaic of tiles of glass and debris
Kissed in a single fading memory
The end of cold night so abreast to the melody

Apology
by Elizabeth Garcia

Funny how easy it was to love you
When you ignored me
Forgot me
Passed me over
I was looking out for you, worrying
And you didn't seem to notice
It was so easy to love you then
Silent and alone
I could imagine a future of my own design
One where you carried on cultivated conversation
And made me blush
Kisses in the rain that never fell
It was so easy, loving my vision
My dream of what you could become
Instead of who you were
That was my fault, and I am sorry
Sorry that I missed the chance to love you
As you are

Friends of the Heart
by Abigail Stroud

We were friends, that's all that used to matter,
Something in between forced our friendship to shatter.
What happened, did we just keep moving forward?
Meet new people, or over the years grow bored?
We each changed throughout the night,
When we awoke the next day and didn't know each other, we put it out of sight.
We grew up, that's all there is to say,
Let go of the things we clenched to yesterday.
We pushed away familiarity and closed our mind,
Starting new journeys, hoping something else we would find.
And it really scampered by fast,
A clock of destruction, erasing our past.
But together we went through so very much,
So I know without doubt we will distantly stay in touch.
Somehow I'm sure that to each other we will always be a friend,
We swore at the beginning, it would last until the end.
We got older, that's all there is to tell,
That's when our friendship steadily fell.
I can't really say what it was that drove us apart,
But you my dear friends, will forever remain in my heart.

Symptoms
by Mariah Iverson-Jones

Slowly walking
hostile staring
the sun arising.
Changes being made
overcoming my heartache.
Calm less smiles step, tick, one inch at a time.
They are waiting for you to come back.
Their figure
no one
knows how it's made.
Possibly preserving the useless,
needing ness,
before escalating.
Imagine.
Breathe.
Break free.
Set loose.
Run with the creatures,
down a path, dark to light.
Bring it back.

Lost In a Fantasy
by Erica Frey

He said he thought that she was pretty
Her heart began to sing
She promised that she would search the city
If he ever asked her to do such a thing
She was a fool for his love that was not alive
She thought she would die without his touch
But he made her believe he would help her survive
Oh he made her believe too much
A sudden goodbye would bring her tears
She still grew fond of him each day
Refusing to accept what she most feared
Thinking he would return and take the pain away
A hello, a glance or a smile would make her see
What she wanted to believe inside her fantasy

My Tree
by Korryn Downey

My tree stood at the top of a hill
It stood with elegance and grace
I would never let it go to the mill
The way it put a smile on my face
But I couldn't protect it forever
And soon the horrible men came
I should have never said never
My poor tree will never be the same
The entire forest was taken down
The family of trees was killed
Soon the land became a town
Her home had been filled
I sit one day where it used to be
Let no one forget my perfect little tree

Never Giving Up
by Shantel Patterson

I'm weak without you, I don't want to do you,
I tend to complain so much but what would I do without you
I try to fill my life with many virtues
Love Peace Kindness Joy and Self Control
But I tend to unfold
Many people ask me: don't praising God get old? Basically asking me
when are you going to give up?
I just laugh at them and hold my head up knowing in my heart
I'm never going to give up.
Knowing when times get hard and I feel down and alone I can call on Jesus
because He's my friend to the end and when I'm walking with him
I know I'll never give up then.
Why would I give up on someone who never gave up on me?
Why would I give up on someone who I can't see
but the way He softened my heart makes me believe?
And not only the holy words He speaks.
But it's a way I feel I'm telling you God's love is for real
So I will never give up.
I will keep my head up
Even if I get fed up
Even if I'm sick lost and confused
I'm never going to give up

Black and White
by Anna Haggerty

Black and white
The checkered wonder,
Black and white
The race of color.
Distinct in snow,
Pure inside,
Mysterious boldness
Of one's outside.
The phantom's mask
Of stolid grace,
The feral voice
It has to taste.
Its aberration
Of right from wrong,
Its exquisite structure
Made up from song.
Black and white
Like pencil and paper,
Black and white
Like all our neighbors.

Boy Arachnid
by Ashley Stant

One look in his coffee stained eyes
And she was ensnared in his web of lies
A girl who had never been in love
Thought he was sent from above
His venom burrowed its way deep into her soul
And that's when he began to take control
When doubt became present in her mind
All of his threads started to unwind
His iron facade started to rust
As all his love revealed itself to be only lust
She said no
And forced him to go
Her first flame died
And she doesn't remember how long she cried
However she is now stronger
And will no longer
Be one of those flies
Who get trapped in a spider's lies

Conflictions
by Dennis Moffitt

I am your friend
And I am your enemy,
I am nice
And I am mean,
I am a saint,
And I am Satan,
I stand
Yet I am sitting,
I argue
Yet I agree,
I am strong
And I am weak.
What does this mean?
I am a friendly enemy,
I treat you good and yet I put you down
I follow God and disobey the world
I stand for what I believe
Yet I sit by you
I argue for what I know
But I agree in a different light
I am mentally strong
And I am physically weak

Imagination
by Maxwell Buls

A completely empty city
Abraham Lincoln without pity
Romeo without Juliet
Your home with no toilet
If money was backed by lead
Another person's thoughts in your head
Playing baseball with no equipment only hands
A worker's union with no demands
A polar bear in your front lawn
A game of chess with out a single pawn
Can you imagine a world without imagination?
A world with no desire or temptation.

Spring's Truth
by Richard Buka III

With Truth, Passion Blooms
Amongst Twisting Violet Hues–
Soothing Rain Falls Down

Remains ...
by Amitie Hylton

Theater shoot downs
in quiet
Miniature worlds
where snow globes
implode perfect realities
It's hard watching painted white faces
grow coldly pale
Suffering
is Nature's first instinct

You
by Timothy Madzey

You
A simple and trivial word
Yet more majestic than all other earthly desires
Three letters binding destiny with love's cords
And searing its image on the wings of angels
Gazing down from the heavens they see your eyes
Children of the skies enviously watching your shimmering grace
Anger, Jealousy, Lust, and Greed
Light infected by darkness
You being the envoy of the chaos
Stars rain down, burning glistening plains across the Earth
Worlds collide and galaxies shatter into the black of night
Yet you still stand
Spires of gold radiate around you
A beacon in the darkest of times
You being the bringer of the dawn
Sewing love's fragile cords around the destiny of another
Binding that one with love's tender kiss
Simple yet majestic
You

I'm Home
by Holly Fredrickson

Timeless voices corrupting my thoughts.
Broken promises led me astray.
Dreaded words released from your lips-
A scripture embedded in my heart as i bleed
A darkening sight but I never feel alone when you're holding me.
I'm with you. I'm Home.

This Is Spring
by Jenna Fox

This is spring
Its beauty and splendor
Should make everyone stop
To enjoy and remember
That this world does not
Belong to only one person.
It belongs to us all.
So please think about this,
Take a moment to pause.
This world needs your help.
Devote to its cause.

I Don't Understand
by Ryan O'Neal

I don't understand why?
I don't understand why it's sad to cry.
I don't understand why friends say hi.
I don't understand why angers cause so much pain.
I don't understand why no one seems so sane.
Why? What are we supposed to do here.
We sit in this world, feeling whatever the next person feels.
So why?
I don't understand why we can't laugh when we cry
I don't understand why friends don't have to say hi.
I don't understand why anger doesn't have to cause so much pain.
I don't understand why we all could just be sane.
Do you?

Forbidden Love
by Camillia Epps

The love we have is strong
Or is this feeling I'm feeling wrong
I can't go over there, he can't come over here
What shall I do, shed a tear?
We communicate with our eyes
But fate says it's all lies
Why do we have to be put through this torture?
Why do they want to steal our rapture?
Why can't they just ratify our love?
Why don't we escape and fly away like doves?
The air that I breathe is toxic
You all say I should be glad but instead I'm frantic
The love that we have is strong
Please don't tell me it's wrong
My soul, my heart, it longs for you
But still there is nothing we can do
The love we have has to be hidden
Because everyone says it's forbidden

I Am
by Kerista Johnson

I am sad and alone.
I wonder if there is really someone out there.
I hear people whispering.
I see people staring as I walk by.
I want to be happy and self-assured.
I am sad and alone.
I pretend to show,
I feel insecure and unloved.
I touch the soul of my heart.
I worry of what others may think.
I cry for acceptance and understanding.
I am sad and alone.
I understand I might be different.
I say, "Be true to yourself."
I dream of having true friends.
I try not to live my life as a lie.
I hope that I will be accepted one day.
I am sad and alone.

Horribly Cliché
by Mikayla Keener

That one smile that pulls on his lips
Showing the dimples engraved in his cheeks
Flashing in my mind like video clips
Leaving me feeling nothing but meek
It all feels horribly cliché
Written like a fairytale
Or a Shakespeare play
Will the happy ending prevail?
A stomach butterfly flutters
At the sight of his face
Listening to the words he mutters
Hoping in his heart I'll find a place
Will this ever pass
Will this feeling last

Forbidden Fruit
by Miranda Patterson

She knows the consequences
but the temptation is stronger.
She tries not to give in
but she can't take it any longer.
"Do it," the serpent hisses.
"There is nothing to lose."
Take it or leave it.
Which one will she choose?
"I can't." she says,
but her flesh beckons her to it.
The serpent stands watching,
chanting, "Do it! Do it!"
The pressure grows stronger
until she finally gives in.
The serpent slithers off
cheerful for his win.
Realizing her mistake,
she looks to the sun.
And hides from her Father,
thinking, "What have I done?"

Our Sunday Best
by Olivia Golemgeske

It hit 32 degrees, and mother started to fill with us.
She grew and grew.
Her sisters along with her.
They started to cover the sky;
to steal all the sun's warmth for us.
Then the day came.
Mother and her sisters became too full to go on.
With love and tenderness,
mother dressed each of us in our warmest and whitest Sunday Best.
She said it was too cold to not be dressed.
When we where all ready mother opened her hand and blew us away.
Hundreds of us slowly falling to a freezing earth.
As we fell our Grandmother whispered the secret in out ears ...
We too will be clouds one day.

I Am
by John Brown

I am obnoxious and gloomy
I wonder when I'm going to die
I hear no faith at all
I see many dead people
I want to have more friends
I am Obnoxious and Gloomy
I pretend that I care
I feel like I'm being watched
I touch nothing, because I have no hands
I worry what is to become of me
I cry myself to sleep often
I am Obnoxious and Gloomy
I understand I must try harder
I say I will reach my goals
I dream about life being easy
I try to set a higher bar
I hope one day I will be successful
I am Obnoxious and Gloomy

Riddle Me This
by Alex Lohrbach

Stuck in time
Just like the Hatter
Spewing out nonsense
But then the teapot clamors
Forbidden from singing
Into exile I roam
But my banishment sent me into my six o'clock dome
Eyes opened or closed
Up above me she rests
Why is a raven like a writing desk?
I have no real answer
Inside me he ticks
I look down the table
A new brain to pick
I dance and I hurdle
Down the runway I flew
Happy happy unbirthday, unbirthday to you

Disappear
by Chelsea Devine

My Vampire Bride will you dance will me tonight?
And share a kiss for a glimpse of the life we left behind?
So many long years ago
When love appeared in life
We were happy as any other
Just being together
Now, I'm afraid, my dear
For part of me has died
And has left you here all alone
My lovely Valentine
Forgive me that this is so
I tried so hard not to let you go
But try as I might it's all in vain
For I will never love again
Fear the curse
That falls on your lovers
Dear child once mine
Hold nothing dear for it appears
That all things eventually Disappear

Stay Strong
by Avian Schmigiel

You aren't "good enough" ...
Life is way too tough.
You're asking "Why? Oh, why?"
You always sigh and cry.
I know life makes you sad
And at times it makes you mad,
But stay strong,
Carry on,
And just keep singing your song.

In the Wake
by Zachary Huff

Ten – Terrain moves and shapes the earth.
Nueve – Night's moon shines bright with a bubbling mirth.
Huit – Heavy snow falls on the streets of the cities.
Sete – Souls wake up to begin singing apologies.
Roku – Red stained waves bring tears to their eyes.
Pyat' – Passersby quickly come down from their highs.
Sì – Spiders spin their webs in perfect time.
Thala:thah – Threatening desert sways into the rhyme.
Zwei – Zipping through the sky, fly birds of a feather.
Uno – Unified, the world comes together.

I Do
by Samantha White

My dreams are filled with future things to be
Each and every day that comes and goes
Is a day that I continue to grow
So close we are yet still far from being free
Although I'm young I have much to see
I have so many secrets that I must show
How time seems to move so slow I don't know
You know my heart is yours, you have the key
I cannot describe all the ways I feel
Once I am free we will not need to hide
When I saw you I knew it was my cue
You've trapped my in those gentle arms of steel
No longer will I deal with mother's chides
I can't wait for the day I say "I Do"

You Taught Me
by Rachel Peterson

You taught me how to walk.
You taught me how to talk.
You taught me wrong from right.
You taught me to never give up without a fight.
You taught me how to cook.
You even taught me how to read a book.
You taught me how to swing a bat.
You always told me to wipe my feet on the mat.
You taught me how to add.
You told me when I was being bad.
You taught me to become a good kid.
You told me to close the lid.
You taught me it's okay to cry.
You taught me to always try.
You taught me to play like a team.
You taught me to always follow my dream.
You taught me to be the best I can be.
But most importantly you taught me to be me.

The Place
by Jasilynn Nelson

There is a place where life begins
It is the place where life can end
This is the place where the sick come
It is the place we want to leave from
There is a place that is always freezing cold
It is the place for the young and old
Some could call it home
While some live here alone
Others come and visit
But it's not because they miss it
Some come here to work
Others come and make smirks
There is a place that's nice and neat
Where lots of families come and meet
This is a place everyone has seen
Where you can find people that are mean
This is a place where miracles happen
But that doesn't mean that bad things can't happen

Fall
by Ernesto Rivas

Leaves Changing colors
Wind, moving trees side to side
fall is here to stay

Secrets and the Night
by Alyssa Langenbrunner

The music echoes off the walls,
fills lyrics in my head,
words with meaning to explain,
all the words I haven't said.
My heart is yearning to find release,
of the emotions I've let build up,
and envies the music's flow,
and wishes it was enough.
The night, to me, seems quiet,
but the stars, they sing a song,
it ends with the sun arising,
to again bring all that's wrong.
So in unease I will awake,
unable to shed a tear,
for the loss of missed, un-ended dreams,
and the coming day I fear.

A Dragon's Nightmare
by T.J. Thompson

A soul trapped in a saurian prison,
The madness of his mind, no rhyme or reason.
With wings cut off by an enemy's blade,
How could a spirit not dwindle or fade.
Long curved talons grasping the floor,
Fangs grinding down till there is no more.
His elongated neck chained to a wall,
A fire breathing mouth unable to call.
Tears roll down his scaly skin,
Over bleeding wounds that cannot mend.
A sad sight of this great beast,
For savages now are about to feast.

I Am a Window
by Brennen Albrecht

I was brought through man's machine
Into walls I fit between
I show only what is true
Down to earth or sky blue
I am a window
I can show outside a place
See the reflection of your face
You can see the seasons from the past
As if they will forever last
In the winter watch the snow
Watch the summer waters flow
I am a window
But outside me you can see
A dark and scary mystery
White and black start to clash
With a swift lightning slash
I fall onto the darkened lawn
Now I am forever gone
I am not a window

Grounded
by Kelsey Jonassen

Take a deep breath, away I go
Above the trees, the wind will blow.
I spread my wings and soar through the sky
On cloud nine, I'm flying high.
Endless fresh air above mountain tops
The tingling feeling of warm raindrops.
I close my eyes and move with grace
On Earth below, I see no face.
The sun is hot and the sky full of light
But when darkness comes, I'll own the night
Back down I go, around and around
Not meant to fly, I was born to the ground.
Hard to believe, how can it be?
My trip of flight, is now just a memory.

Mesmeric Poetry
by Ayshia Grimes

You speak in melodic tones;
So indescribable, unrecognizable and unknown.
I'm engulfed in the definition.
My mind swims in its dimensions with depths like an ocean;
It's so open, but what does it mean?
Is it hidden beneath the sea?
Unheard and unseen.
In sync as an intricate whirlpool of words;
Creating individual thoughts.
They understand each other as if it were a plot.
Discretely uniting as one.
A creation of harmony leaving its victims in a transfixed position.

Letting Go
by Kontessa Kinsey

Holding on hurts,
Letting go is hard,
Shedding tears helps,
To get away hopeless,
Life follows you as you follow it.
You want away, but you can't run.
Walking seems frustrating, but no one can run forever.
You have to slow down, calm down, and be the runner, but also the winner.
Don't be stuck in last place because you're still at the starting line.

Blasphemy
by Jackie Pollo

And in the reign of unobstructed sovereignty
Such storms and rage untamed
Will saturate in acceptance
Or smother in wreak hostility
Our consciences remain unblamed
For sins we wrought without repentance.

Twilight
by Hannah Blubaugh

The sun begins to set
Amber washes over the land
Creatures of light start to fret-
Twilight is at hand
The messengers of dark appear
Seizing their unsuspecting prey
Losing everything so dear
As the world turns to grey
Our young hero tries to save
All the creatures of the light
He, so strong, clever and brave
Full of courage for the fight
But not even he can be saved
From this nameless evil, twilight
And with his human form depraved
Turns to a blue-eyed beast, black as night
As the world returns to its former self
With evil vanquished across the land
The mysterious twilight is always felt
For twilight is always at hand

A.B.G.
by Jaren Snyder

I want to succeed but don't know how,
I thought I could do it on my own, but I am alone now.
Making that mistake of telling her bye,
I felt cold and distraught like a migrated butterfly.
Not knowing what's next in life for me,
I move from flower to flower like a bee.
Not caring for anyone's feelings but my own,
I'm missing the girl that I talked to every night on the phone.
Feeling like an insensitive jerk,
Being with her had a huge perk.
Just calling her my own and having her by my side,
Made me realize that I ruined everything like a high tide.
Destroying everything in its way,
I will never forget the moment of that day.
But enough of the sad times and on to the good,
If I could go back to the first night we met, I would.

Jonathon Barnett

Emotions
by Jonathon Barnett

Anger builds behind this dam.
It boils and writhes and takes no form.
The dam bursts, blurring who I am.
The connections I made seem forever torn.
Pain strikes hard and fast at my core.
They say it's only weakness leaving my body,
But it invades and rips down my door.
While behind it comes a shape, walking calmly.
Hope stands among the splintered wood,
Reaching down with a soft, perfect hand;
Her light washes away the searing flood.
I accept her grasp as she helps me stand.
But Loss rushes by stealing Hope from my arms.
Grief, an ugly, wretched woman, takes her place.
She whispers lies into my ears, "All but I will do you harm!"
My thoughts become corrupt, my words leave a sour taste.
A new light appears, a brighter light than e'er before.
This light I know nobody can take.
Love steps in and limb from limb Grief is torn.
A smile fills my heart, I know I'll always be safe

2nd Place

Chandler Ellison

Dawn
by Chandler Ellison

Dawn is no dove
No gentle wings,
No melodious words,
Wrath rekindled
Decisive dawn
Severing the night
A guillotine,
Death bringer to darkness
Lighting the sky
Aflame
A raging inferno
To crown the day
Dawn
The revolutionary
Free, free
The world!
No merciful morning
No tiptoeing peace
Rise, rise
The falcon, Dawn

Sinnea Douglas

Now in her last year of high school,
Sinnea plans to attend college
where she will study English, Creative Writing, and Journalism,
in hopes of one day becoming an English teacher and published author.
This talented senior has been writing for four years,
with her deep love of language providing her with inspiration.
We are thrilled to be able to help at least one of her dreams come true
as it gives us great pleasure to present the work of Sinnea Douglas,
published author, and winner of this year's Editor's Choice Award.

Editor's Choice Award

Motherhood
by Sinnea Douglas

These days I drench my dreams in
teething rings, turkey sandwich lunches,
school plays, and sports teams.
   Hang them up like southern laundry and wait for the scenes to play.

And across sheets of time - I see you -
A Bundle of Poetry waiting to be spoken.
Your laughter - Jazz trickling from tiny spit bubbles.
Your beauty - Lines of simile tightly entwined into locks of wavy hair.
Your life - a motion picture whose release date has been threatened.
But I've already purchased the tickets
   I know better.

      I need you my child,
      beautiful as the footprints the sun leaves across the evening sky.

      I need you my child,
      as real as the congas that beat in my chest.
      You will breathe that first breath. No matter what they say.

God himself sculpted you from the clouds,
Dipped His brush into starlight, and painted you into my womb.
And this womb
   will be a tomb to no child.

Index
of
Authors

Index of Authors

Index of Authors

Index of Authors

Index of Authors

Acclaimed

Price List

Initial Copy 32.95

Additional Copies 24.00

Please Enclose $6 Shipping/Handling Each Order
Must specify book title and author

Check or Money Order Payable to:

The America Library of Poetry
P.O. Box 978
Houlton, Maine 04730

Please Allow 4-6 Weeks For Delivery

THE AMERICA
LIBRARY OF POETRY

www.libraryofpoetry.com

Email: generalinquiries@libraryofpoetry.com